Art treasures of Florence
museums, churches, refectories, palaces and itineraries

FIRENZE
MVSEI

Ilaria Taddei

Art treasures

of Florence

museums, churches, refectories, palaces

and itineraries

s i l l a b e

© 2000 Ministero per i Beni e le Attività Culturali -
    Soprintendenze di Firenze

A publication of

s i l l a b e s.r.l.
Livorno
http://www.sillabe.it

managing editor: Maddalena Paola Winspeare
graphic design: Laura Belforte
translation: Anthony Cafazzo
editing: Bettina Müller

photographs: Archivio Sillabe: Foto Remo Bardazzi, Foto Paolo Nannoni
Archivio Fotografico SBAA Firenze, Archivio Fotografico SBAS Firenze,
Archivio Giunti, Archivio Mandragora, Giuseppe d'Abruzzo,
Nicolò Orsi Battaglini

photolithography: La Nuova Lito - Firenze; Studiolito - Città di Castello

Cover: Verrocchio and Leonardo da Vinci, *Baptism of Christ*, Uffizi

ISBN 88-8347-018-4

Contents

One must begin with the Uffizi; not because it is the most important museum in Florence; nor because it holds the ultimate expression of our figurative culture, Giotto and Michelangelo, Leonardo and Caravaggio. No, one must begin with the Uffizi because only by traversing it from beginning to end may one understand the true and unique character of this city, not to mention the title of this book-cum-guide that I introduce to you here.

There is a suggestion that I always make to anyone either arriving in Florence for the first time or staying only a short while: go straight to the Uffizi and walk through it, slowly. Never mind the Giottos and Michelangelos, the Leonardos and Caravaggios; you will return to the Uffizi again; there will be other occasions to take pause before these masterpieces. For now, limit yourselves to strolling through the corridors, very slowly, guided by the sole pleasure of looking. To the left is a procession of archaeological statues and rooms opening onto the utmost expressions of painting, to the right, the Dome of Brunelleschi, the Tower of Arnolfo di Cambio, the roofs and bell towers of the city, the foreshortening of Piazza della Signoria and Orcagna's Loggia with its sculptures, the fountain, the grand duke on horseback. Once you have reached the short wing of the Uffizi, a veritable balcony overlooking the city, observe what extends before you - the river crossed by bridges as tense as arches, the Belvedere hill, dense with villas and churches, the bell tower of Santo Spirito, the harmonious line of the riverside "Lungarni", the forms of this city cut like a precious jewel from the Tuscan matrix.

At this point, you will have understood two fundamental things (and herein lie the keys to making best use of this book and understanding both the spirit motivating it and the logic governing it).

You will have understood, above all, that Florence is indeed the *city of the Uffizi*, in the sense that this, its greatest museum, crosses it like a bridge, while at the same time, the city 'enters' tangibly within its walls. The beauty that inhabits the museum spreads forth into the city squares and streets; it is transformed into the landscape of the hills and the profile of the bridges; it takes the shape of domes and bell towers and is echoed in the colours of the stone and plaster.

Equally as important, you will have understood that the beauty of Florence is made up of mirroring and equilibrium: the masterpieces of painting are reflected in the colours and shape of the city. The ones would not exist without the others. To violate the geometry of Florentine roofs would be to violate the *Battle of San Romano* by Paul Uccello; if Brunelleschi's dome were different, so would Botticelli.

Florence holds it all together: the art of the city must be understood and known as a unitary whole (first understanding and then knowledge). Afterwards, it will be easier to move about within the variegated compendium of sites and circumstances. Such is the art Florence offers, an offering that, on first impact, may baffle and intimidate.

Consider the extraordinary variety of museums. Nowhere else does anything comparable exist. In fact, what other city has transformed the *cenacoli* of ancient convents into a series of museums? And where else does a collection exist comparable to that of the *Opificio delle Pietre Dure?* - the ancient Medici artisan shop still active and famous throughout the world for its restoration work - a collection that is at once a document of industrial archaeology, a precious mineralogical sampling and a splendid tribute to State art in its highest expression. What other major Italian or European city can boast such a wide and outstanding series of museums linked to the names of famous collectors, antiquarians and art historians? It is enough just to name the Bardini, Horne, Stibbert and Davanzati Museums, the collections of Contini Bonacossi, Salvatore Romano and Alberto della Ragione, and the Berenson and Longhi Foundations, let alone the monographic museums, that is, those dedicated to the life and work of single artists (for instance, the Museum of San Marco and Casa Buonarroti), the specialist museums (the Silver works, Porcelain and Carriage Museums on the Pitti Palace grounds, the *Gabinetto dei Disegni e delle Stampe* of the Uffizi (Drawing and Print Office), the plasters of Porta Romana, the ancient musical instruments already in the Cherubini Conservatory and now in the process of being transferred to the Accademia) or the rich, though insufficiently appreciated universe of the science museums.

And then there are the private *palazzi* that still harbour celebrated collections, the cloisters, convents, gardens and the resplendent churches of Florence.

Ten books the size of this one would probably still not suffice to speak of everything, to thoroughly address the many aspects of art in Florence.

What has been possible, however, is to delineate some routes, to select some significant themes and to propose a method of reading the art you will see, so as to allow you to come to an understanding of the overall splendour and significance of the anomaly that is Florence.

In my opinion, Ilaria Taddei has managed laudably in this, and I am certain that the reader will appreciate her worthy efforts.

Antonio Paolucci
Head of the Fine Arts and Historic
Works Commission of Florence, Pistoia and Prato

This handy volume represents a quick, yet exhaustive guide to visiting Florence. It provides detailed information, not only on the city's universally renowned sights, but on many other of its most representative works as well. It is divided into two sections: the first presents concise, authoritative descriptions of the monuments and works of art arranged according to category (museums, churches, refectories with Last Suppers and palaces); the second guides the reader through itineraries of various geographical areas of the city, referring to the detailed descriptions contained in the first section.

MUSEUMS

THE UFFIZI

It was duke Cosimo I de' Medici who wished to move and consolidate in a single building all the Magistrature, that is to say, the administrative and judicial 'offices' (i.e., Uffizi). He entrusted the project to Georgio Vasari, the architect who had at the duke's request already overseen the work of restructuring and enlarging Palazzo della Signoria (p. 126). The first stone of the new building was laid in 1560. Five years later, on the occasion of the wedding of Cosimo's son, Francesco, with Johanna of Austria, Vasari completed, in only five months of work, the corridor that would unite the two centres of power, the new Medici residence in Pitti Palace (p. 100-101) and Palazzo della Signoria (p. 126). In 1580, when neither the duke who commissioned it, nor the architect who designed it were alive to see it, the new Uffizi were inaugurated. Its U-shaped layout surrounded the romanesque church of San Pier Scheraggio and the Mint (Palazzo della Zecca). In 1581 Francesco I ordered ancient sculptures and portraits to be placed on the top floor of the east wing, beneath the ceiling frescoed in grotesque figures by Alessandro Allori and assistants. However, the true treasure of the Medici collection was set in the Gallery designed by Bernardo Buontalenti (as was the Theatre) that took up part of the first and second floors, as well as the hanging gardens in the Loggia of Palazzo della Signoria. A foundry and other artisan workshops found their place in the building's other wing. Over the centuries, the various collections grew to include, not only paintings and sculptures, but armour, scientific instrumentation, bronze and gold work as well. In the late 18th Century the collections were rearranged according to the cannons of the Age of Enlightenment, a reordering that carried on into the following century. This led to a collection that would earn the Uffizi its place amongst the world's most important picture galleries. Its holdings include, not only some extraordinary paintings, amongst which the unique series of self-portraits deserves special mention, but also exquisite sketches and miniatures.

ANDREA DEL CASTAGNO

Illustrious Men Frescoes (Queen Tomyris)
circa 1449-1450
Church of San Pier Scheraggio

This series of frescoes was painted in the mid 15th Century by Andrea del Castagno for the Carducci villa in Legnaia, on the outskirts of Florence. Together with the Sibyl Cumana and two queens of antiquity, Esther and Tomyris, the painter sets six important personages of Florentine history and culture: the valiant condottiere, Pippo Spano, the Ghibelline, Farinata degli Uberti, the banker, Niccolò Acciaioli and the three most eminent representatives of Italian literature, Dante, Boccaccio and Petrarch. In keeping with a medieval iconographic tradition of Nordic origins transposed onto the humanistic climate prevailing at the time, the artist proposes the glorious characters of both the distant and recent past as models of virtue to be emulated. They are depicted as statues set in niches, and are meant to appear as such in their plastic aspect. They are exhibited in the nave of the romanesque Church of San Pier Scheraggio, consecrated in 1068 and the centre of Guild meetings until Palazzo dei Priori was built. After the left aisle was demolished in the early 15th Century, (some arches are still visible in Via della Ninna), the church was incorporated by Vasari into the Uffizi in 1560.

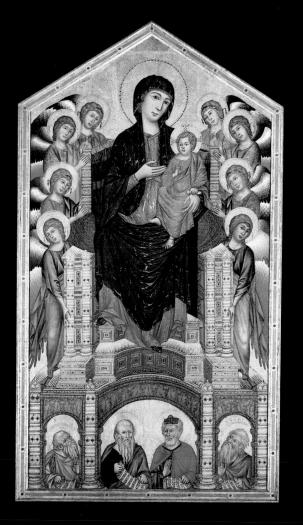 

CIMABUE
Santa Trinita Maestà
1280-1290

DUCCIO DI BONINSEGNA
Maestà
circa 1285

GIOTTO
Ognissanti Madonna
circa 1310

Room 2

This room, which with its trussed roof recalls the nave of a medieval church, holds the three great wood panels representing the Maestà, that is, the Virgin Mary enthroned as Queen of the Heavens presenting the Child Jesus, hand raised in a blessing to the faithful. Cimabue's painting (to the right) was found on the main altar of the Church of Santa Trinita and is the oldest, showing the influence of Byzantine art in the gold highlighting of the mantle's folds. Duccio di Boninsegna, the Sienese painter who was strongly influenced by Cimabue's work, made the panel to the left (still in its original frame) for the Laudesi confraternity chapel in Santa Maria Novella: the penchant for sinuous contour lines was wholly new at the time. Lastly, it was Giotto who executed the central Maestà for the altar to the right of the partition door in the Church of Ognissanti. The saints, together with the angels, are rendered in a space that has a true-to-life depth. The volumetric compactness of the Madonna seated on the marble throne, similar to the coeval tabernacles by Arnolfo di Cambio, hints at the contour of her body beneath the robes.

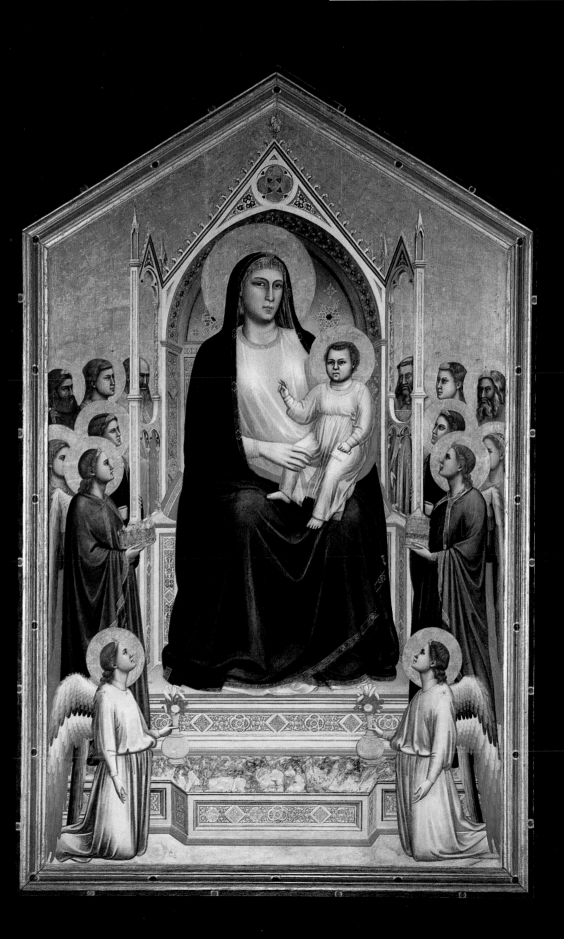

SIMONE MARTINI AND LIPPO MEMMI

Annunciation
1333
Room 3

This work, one of the most significant of 14th-century Italian art, was painted by Simone Martini and his brother-in-law Lippo Memmi for the altar of Sant Ansano in the Siena Cathedral. A neo-gothic frame has replaced the original one, which was lost, as was the central tondo (or roundel), probably with God the Father, while the authors' signatures and the date inscribed (1333) are original. Sant'Ansano and Saint Margaret (?) are depicted on either side of the *Annunciation*, while the tondi hold four prophets with scrolls. Spatial depth is suggested, firstly, by the movement imparted by the sinuous line (consummately Sienese) of the Virgin's mantle as she withdraws timidly in the face of the angel's announcement, then by the foreshortened detail of the book in her hand, and finally by the lily-filled vase placed on the veined marble floor in the centre of the background plane in order to divide the scene. The trailing tartan mantle of the angel gives one the sense that it has just landed, and the judicious use of gold clearly reveals its unearthly provenance.

GENTILE DA FABRIANO

Adoration of the Magi
1423
Rooms 5-6

While the principles of renaissance art were being established, Gentile da Fabriano, protagonist of the international gothic (an artistic movement linked to courtly culture), painted the *Adoration of the Magi* in 1423 (as appears on the picture's frame). It had been commissioned by the rich and scholarly merchant, Palla Strozzi, who intended it for the family chapel in Santa Trinita, restructured by Lorenzo Ghiberti. This latter artist's architecture is reflected in the elaborate cuspidate frame (which bears flowers painted from life in its artificial pillars), the procession of the Magi in the upper portion of the tripartite space and the scene of the Adoration in the foreground. Through the sparkling colours and profusion of gold (also on the modelled plaster portions in relief), the eyes course through the single episodes and are held by the myriad details, in analogy to the *ekphrasis* – the description of artworks according to the literary cannons of Greek humanism, of which Strozzi was an avid exponent, so much so that he financed the first chair of the Greek language at the University of Florence.

MASACCIO AND MASOLINO

Saint Anne Metterza
circa 1424
Room 7

This is a collaborative work by Masolino and Masaccio, datable to around 1424, when the two painters were commissioned to do the frescoes of the Brancacci Chapel (p. 161). Masolino has been credited with Saint Anne and all the angels except the green-clothed one at the upper right, which instead is most likely by Masaccio, author as well of the Madonna and Child. The latter two figures are designed in perspective and with a sculptural solidity that, in the Herculean Child, becomes a punctilious reference to classical art. Traditional iconography calls for the Madonna to be sitting in her mother Anne's lap and a Child Jesus of comparatively smaller dimensions. In this work, whose title (*Met-terza* from the medieval Latin "equal third") alludes to this kinship, the figure of Saint Anne, with her ample mantle – like the dome that Brunelleschi was erecting in those years – becomes the loving, protecting mother of Mary. The painting comes from Sant' Ambrogio, a Benedictine monastery whose nuns owed, according to "the Rule", filial obedience to the mother superior.

Paolo Uccello
Battle of San Romano
Dated to between circa 1435-1438 or circa 1456-1460
Room 7

This painting, as revealed by the 1492 inventory of the furnishings, was found in the room of Lorenzo il Magnifico in the Medici palace in Via Larga together with two others panels today in the London National Gallery and the Louvre. All three works address the triumph of the Florentines over the Sienese, allied with the Visconti, at San Romano in Valdelsa on June 1, 1432. In particular, the work in the Uffizi, signed by Paul Uccello on one of shields on the ground, depicts the episode of the unsaddling of Bernardino della Ciarda, head of the enemy troops, by Niccolò da Tolentino, the Florentine condottiere portrayed as well by Andrea del Castagno in Santa Maria del Fiore (p. 141). The battle unfolds in a tangle of armoured men (originally in silver leaf), animals and weapons, as if suspended in time through a sophisticated exercise in perspective. Although there is no doubt that the work was commissioned by Cosimo il Vecchio, when it was commissioned appears less certain: immediately after the victory or later, toward 1460; in which case, the work would be linked to the philosophical and ethical thinking of Seneca so dear to Cosimo.

Piero della Francesca,
Triumphs of Battista and Federico, rear of the Dukes of Urbino diptych

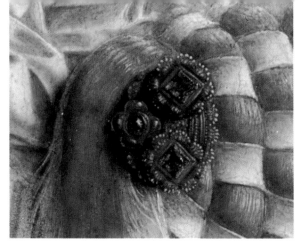

THE UFFIZI

Piero della Francesca
Diptych of the dukes of Urbino
circa 1472
Room 7

The diptych, which was once hinged and opened like a book, reached Florence in 1631 through the inheritance of Vittoria della Rovere, Ferdinando II de' Medici's bride and last descendant of the dukes of Urbino. The profile of Battista Sforza, who at the age of only fourteen married Federico, duke of Urbino, appears in all its clarity, vividly illuminated by the light reflected in the jewels adorning her. Federico's portrait faces her, slightly in shadow, through which the artist has outlined his particular physiognomy with great precision. Renowned condottiere and refined benefactor, Federico built his fortune on the exploits of his mercenary troops. He is portrayed here with geometric rigor in the red garb of the renaissance gentleman. The two portraits are united by the same background landscape, over which the light of a clear autumn day extends. On the back of the diptych, the *Triumphs* of Battista and Federico underscore the commemorative intent of the work. Sitting on a wagon drawn by unicorns, symbolising chastity, the duchess is surrounded by the Theological Virtues. Federico in armour rides in a wagon drawn by white horses, while winged Victory crowns him with laurel and the Cardinal Virtues sit before him. The diptych was likely painted after the death of the duchess during childbirth in 1472, as can be inferred from the inscription, a sort of funeral eulogy, found beneath the triumph of Battista.

17

FILIPPO LIPPI

Madonna and Child with two angels
circa 1465
Room 8

The noble, sweetly profiled Madonna sits on an opulent throne, while two angels uplift the plump Child Jesus. In this late work by Filippo Lippi, which will have such a great influence his student, Botticelli (p. 130), the artist looks to the sculpture of Donatello and Luca della Robbia, while the bird's-eye-view landscape and the meticulously studied women's ornaments are evocative of Flemish painting. The figures of the little children were inspired by popular tradition: note particularly the playful angel in the foreground looking towards the observer, serving almost as a counterpoint to the solemnly rapt expression on Mary's face.

FILIPPINO LIPPI AND COLLABORATORS

Adoration of the Magi
1496
Room 8

In 1481 the Regular Clergy of Saint Augustine asked Leonardo da Vinci to paint an *Adoration of the Magi* to set on the altar of the church of San Donato in Scopeto, just outside Florence's Porta Romana (the church was demolished in 1529 in order to avoid providing shelter to the imperial troops besieging Florence). A long time passed and the altarpiece remained incomplete (p. 25), even up to the Maestro's departure for Milan. It was only in 1496 that the clergymen were able to entrust the charge to Filippino Lippi, who was assisted in the task by another painter, perhaps Piero di Cosimo, as revealed by recent restorations. In the clear skies over a landscape populated by processions of horsemen, crowds of pagans appear on the right following the Magi, rendered in the exotic physiognomy and dress of "Barbarians". The sacred event is revealed to them by the man on the far right wrapped in a yellow mantle, whom the painter portrayed as his friend Piero del Pugliese. On the other side of the painting we find the group in regal dress, portraying the 'popular' Medici, descendants of Lorenzo il Vecchio, following the family tradition that associated them to the Company of the Magi: Pierfrancesco is the genuflecting magician-astronomer with the astrolabe, and behind him are his sons, Giovanni, with a precious vessel, and Lorenzo, with crown removed as a sign of humility before Christ the King.

ANTONIO AND PIERO DEL POLLAIOLO
Saints James, Vincent and Eustace ("Altarpiece of the Cardinal of Portugal")
1466-1468
Room 9

The altarpiece, a collaborative work between Antonio and Piero del Pollaiolo, adorned the altar of the Cardinal of Portugal chapel in the church of San Miniato al Monte (p. 152). It was executed in around 1466, when the body of young Prince Jacopo of Lusitania, who died in Florence, was laid to rest there. Antonio, a goldsmith, engraver and sculptor, often carried out his painting activities together with his younger brother Piero. Although it is difficult to distinguish the hand of one from the other, it would appear that Antonio played the primary role both in designing the work, tending towards lofty composition, and executing the central figure. The main figures are set on a balcony with bronze balustrade and floor inlayed with the same motifs as those in the chapel, filling the entire foreground: in the centre is St. James, namesake of Jacopo, to the left, St. Vincent, patron saint of Lisbon, the prince's native city, and to the right, St. Eustace, titular of the Roman church where he was cardinal. Beyond them extends a bird's-eye-view landscape typical of the Flemish tradition. The panel maintains its magnificent original frame, a rare occurrence that allows us to appreciate the close correspondence between the two components.

SANDRO BOTTICELLI
Adoration of the Magi
circa 1475
Room 10-14

For the altarpiece of the chapel, Guasparre di Zanobi del Lama, broker at the Arte del Cambio, the powerful bankers' guild to which the Medici family also belonged, chose Sandro Botticelli, who had just painted the joust standard for Giuliano de' Medici. The subject, the *Adoration of the Magi*, was in keeping with the chapel's title, dedicated to the Epiphany. However, it was also a theme very dear to the Medici family, who participated in the annual processions of the Company of the Magi, a secular fraternity, dressing as the oriental kings. Thus, depicted in this panel are Cosimo il Vecchio, kneeling in front of Child Jesus, together with his two sons, Piero il Gottoso and Giovanni. Also participating in this sacred event unfolding amongst ancient ruins are other exponents of the Medici house and their dearest friends: to the left, Giuliano, on whom Agnolo Poliziano is leaning, and next to them, Pico della Mirandola, while on the opposite side is Lorenzo, dressed in black, and in the far corner, turned towards the spectator, Botticelli himself.

SANDRO BOTTICELLI

Primavera

circa 1482
Room 10-14

This renowned picture belonged to Lorenzo di Pierfrancesco de' Medici, cousin of Lorenzo il Magnifico, who kept it in the residence in via Larga (p. 185) above a small bed in the same room where Botticelli's *Pallas and the Centaur* hung (now in the Uffizi on the same wall as *Venus*). It was then transferred, together with *The Birth of Venus*, to the villa at Castello where Vasari saw it for the first time and in describing it was to establish the title by which it has been know ever since, Spring. Botticelli painted it just after his return from Rome, where he had completed the Sistine chapel frescoes. The painting expresses the refined culture of the court of Lorenzo il Magnifico, frequented by the neo-Platonic philosopher Marsilio Ficino and the poet Agnolo Poliziano, author of *Le Stanze*, a work that together with the classical texts read in that ambience would inspire the theme of the garden of Venus to the painter. On the picture's right, Zephyrus pursues and takes hold of the nymph Chloris and, after having married her, grants her the power to give birth to flowers (which here in fact flow from her mouth), thus transforming her into Flora, the Roman goddess of Spring. In the centre is Venus with blindfold Cupid, who shoots an arrow toward the group of Graces dancing in a circle in a classical arrangement. Set apart on the left is Mercury, the winged messenger who with his caduceus spreads the clouds of knowledge. The painting can therefore be read as the path from carnal love to spiritual and intellectual love. According to another interpretation – which also sees Spring as represented in the painting – the meaning would be linked to the marriage of Lorenzo di Pierfrancesco to Semiramide d'Appiano in May, 1482. The most recent hypothesis holds that it is an exaltation of the Liberal Arts, according to which the central figure is not Venus, but Philology. Thus shall the picture ever remain a mystery whose beauty attains a universal value beyond all symbolism, even that of the innumerable spring flowers blooming on the hills surrounding Florence.

SANDRO BOTTICELLI

The Birth of Venus

circa 1484
Room 10-14

Botticelli painted this masterpiece in the cultured ambience of the Florentine court of Lorenzo il Magnifico. It is documented by Vasari together with *Primavera* in the Castello villa, country home of Lorenzo di Pierfrancesco de' Medici, cousin of Lorenzo, although it is not certain that this was the painting's original destination, despite canvas supports being used at the time for pagan themes intended for such rural settings. Homer's *Hymn to Venus*, the love poetry of Ovid and the verses of Botticelli's friend, Poliziano, are the likely literary references, together with the figurative ones, such as *Venus pudica* (the chaste), which the painter drew upon for this allegorical fable, whose protagonist is the goddess of love in all her sensual beauty. Driven forward on a shell by Zephyrus and Aura, the spring breezes laden with a perfume to which the roses allude, Venus lands ashore, where a young girl drapes her in a flowered mantle. The figure of the girl has been interpreted as one of the Hours, the goddess' nymphs in waiting, or one of the Graces charged with weaving her mantle.

THE UFFIZI

VERROCCHIO AND LEONARDO DA VINCI
Baptism of Christ
Dated to between 1473 and 1478
Room 15

This wood panel from the church of San Michele a San Salvi epitomises the way works were carried out in a flourishing Renaissance workshop such as that of Verrocchio during the early fourteen-seventies: a team of artists would collaborate on the works commissioned from the shop's maestro. Vasari writes that da Vinci's contribution to the *Baptism* would cause Verrocchio to definitively give up painting, as he felt surpassed by his student. The hand of the young, highly gifted da Vinci has been recognised in the light-suffused angel to the left and the background landscape, but, as confirmed by recent restorations, other artists must have participated in completing the work. The anatomy of the body of the Baptist is drawn with tangible tension, quite different from Christ's sweet, yet steadfast figure, and the palm and rocks behind John the Baptist reveal a clear-cut execution quite distinct from the misty marshland scene.

LEONARDO DA VINCI
Annunciation
Dated to between 1475 and 1480
Room 15

Still under the guidance of Verrocchio, da Vinci executed the *Annunciation* for the church of San Bartolomeo a Monteoliveto. He recalls his maestro in the ornate lectern that echoes the forms of Verrocchio's funeral monument to Piero and Giovanni de' Medici in the Old Sacristy of San Lorenzo (p. 148). The still young da Vinci evidently experienced some difficulty in rendering perspective, as can be appreciated in the right arm of the Virgin, who sits before a stately Tuscan home. His naturalist tendencies are already evident in the flowering garden, the angel's wings and the density effects of the air that, beyond a mantle of dark trees, reveals the landscape paling in the distance to be lost in the mists enveloping a city and mountains, almost suspended on far-away waters.

LEONARDO DA VINCI

Adoration of the Magi

1481
Room 15

It was da Vinci's father, a notary and guarantor of all legal transactions of the convent of San Donato in Scopeto, who played the decisive role in having the commission of this work assigned to young Leonardo in 1481. The painting was left incomplete in the state of a chiaroscuro sketch when the artist departed for Milan the following year. Its completion was then entrusted to Filippino Lippi (p. 18). Awe-stricken bystanders gather round the Madonna and Child. Barely entering into this eventful scene permeated by the mystery of divinity manifest are a proud youth on the right and a meditative man on the left, perhaps Saint Joseph – who according to an apocryphal Gospel stands aside to allow the pagans to behold the mother and child. Following from the same reasoning (i.e., that da Vinci adhered to the descriptions provided in that apocryphal Gospel), a suggestive hypothesis has recently been formulated that gives meaning to the architectural ruins and skirmishing knights in the background. The *Gospel* in fact narrates that the soldiers of Herod clashed with the men accompanying the Magi, and that the building's columns were razed, with consequent great fear and hasty flight on the part of the bystanders.

MICHELANGELO BUONARROTI
Holy Family with Young Saint John ("Tondo Doni")
circa 1507
Room 25

TRIBUNA
Room 18

Francesco I conceived of this Gallery with the same taste for the natural and artificial that he imparted to the *Studiolo* in Palazzo Vecchio (p. 128). It was designed by Bernardo Buontalenti in 1584 as treasure room and hall of wonder, as well as sanctuary for masterpieces of sculpture and painting. The octagonal room presents itself to the visitor all at once in its full splendour, according to a cosmological significance exalting the deeds of the dynasty. In fact, it contains allusions to the four elements: the wind vane and rose on the lantern (air), the mother-of-pearl incrustations on the vault and drum (water), the red velvet on the walls (fire) and the marbles of the floor (earth), to which a frieze painted by Jacopo Ligozzi was added. Originally, even the colours of the Gallery (red, blue and gold) contained a heraldic allusion. The *Tribuna* was profoundly altered by the Lorraine, who had the masterpieces formerly held in the Uffizi transferred here and set in counterpoint to the classical sculptures, for the most part Roman copies of Greek originals, that had become famous since they were placed here at the behest of Cosimo III. Today the painting collection exhibited has been reduced and the original wall tapestries replaced. The walls are now hung with 16th-century Florentine paintings, including many official portraits of the Medici family, while the classical statues have remained surrounding the semi-precious stone table fashioned in the grand duke's workshops.

The only wood panel painting attributed with certainty to Michelangelo, the tondo was made for Agnolo Doni and Maddalena Strozzi, already portrayed by Raphael (p. 110), most likely on the occasion of the birth of their first-born, Maria, on September 8, 1507. The significance of the work would seem related to that joyous event: there are allusions to the Birth of Jesus and his Baptism, such as the young Saint John on the right and the five heads in full relief on the monumental frame, designed by Michelangelo himself and executed by Marco and Francesco del Tasso. It is certain that the painting was carried out after January 1506, when the *Laocoon* group was rediscovered in Rome, because the pose of the nude sitting on the wall behind Joseph is a clear reference to this work, just as the several nudes seem to evoke other Hellenistic sculptures. In the foreground, the group of the *Holy Family*, with a full-bodied Mary in a sinuous pose and an imposing Saint Joseph who are passing the Child. Chronology would therefore set the work in strict relationship to the frescoes of the Sistine chapel – a fact also borne out by the stylistic perspective, given the plastic postures and cold, iridescent colours of the two masterpieces.

RAPHAEL (RAFFAELLO SANZIO)
Madonna and Child with young Saint John ("Madonna of the goldfinch")
circa 1505-1506
Room 26

Raphael executed the painting during his Florentine sojourn in 1505 for the occasion of the wedding of the merchant Lorenzo Nasi. The Child Jesus is depicted nestled between his mother's knees caressing a goldfinch in the hand of the boy Saint John. The wood panel is in a precarious state, as it was heavily damaged in the collapse of the Nasi home in via dei Bardi in 1547, and any reading of the chromatic range is made difficult by the thick layers of varnish and yellowed restorations. In this work, Raphael experiments for the first time with a centralised composition with Mary and the little boys constituting a single, pyramidally structured unit. The Madonna and Child display sweet, absorbed expressions redolent of Perugino, while the landscape, which x-ray studies have shown to have been drawn free-hand with great rapidity, seems influenced by the works of Leonardo da Vinci.

RAPHAEL (RAFFAELLO SANZIO)
Pope Leo X with Cardinals Giulio de' Medici and Luigi de' Rossi
1518
Room 26

This triple portrait arrived in Florence from Rome in September of 1518, just over five years after the election of the Medici pope, Leo X. The painting immediately inspired enthusiastic admiration – the same any today would feel casting eyes upon the miniated code, the engraved silver bell, the chair's knob (alluding to the Medici emblem) reflecting the pope's shoulders and the window, the admirable harmony of the different shades of red, from the dark hue of the velvet to the brilliant damask. Radiographs taken for its restoration revealed a sketch underlying the figure of the pope. No such sketch was instead found for the figures of the two cardinals, which must therefore have been added at a later time. Thus, Giulio Romano, Raphael's student, put his hand to the work, as in fact reported by Vasari, and it is to him we may attribute the harsher lines of Cardinal Luigi de' Rossi at the pope's shoulders, while it was Sebastiano del Piombo who, according to critics, executed Cardinal Giulio de' Medici on the left.

TITIAN (TIZIANO VECELLIO)
Venus of Urbino
1538
Room 28

Commissioned from Titian by the duke of Urbino, Guidubaldo della Rovere in 1538, the painting is probably an allegorical representation of conjugal love, a wedding gift from the duke to his young bride, Giulia Varano. In it a young, completely naked woman lays with lascivious abandon amongst the ruffled sheets of an undone bed – in her right hand, a bouquet of roses, symbol of Venus. The expression on her face, at once sweet and sensual, and the ambivalent unrestraint of her left hand seem an invitation to partake of the pleasures of love, whilst the call to the serenity of connubial life is represented by the little dog, symbol of fidelity, as well as by the maidservants in the background rummaging through the wedding chest. The cloth, the shining pearl on the young girl's ear, as well as her complexion are all rendered with the silky elegance typical of the painting canons of the great Venetian artist. The painting reached Florence in 1631 with the inheritance of Vittoria della Rovere, Ferdinando II de' Medici's wife.

THE NIOBE ROOM
Room 42

In 1770 the sculptural group depicting the myth of Niobe was brought from Rome by Pietro Leopoldo, who entrusted its restoration to Innocenzo Spinazzi. The room chosen to host it in the Uffizi was that at the end of the third corridor, prepared by Gaspare Maria Paoletti and decorated with reliefs by Francesco Carradori and plasters by the Ticino artist, Grato Albertolli (who, together with his brother, Giocondo, had worked on the Sala Bianca in Palazzo Pitti and the Salone delle Feste in the Poggio Imperiale Villa). Copies of original Roman sculptures from the 3rd to 2nd Century BC, they were discovered in Rome in 1583, and acquired by the then cardinal Ferdinando de' Medici, who set them in the Villa Medici garden, while the moulds from which they were cast were sent to Florence. Here, they are arranged together with other statues pertaining to the same myth, according to which, as Ovid narrates, Niobe, proud of his children to the point of claiming them equal to Latona, mother of Apollo and Diana, was punished for his temerity: Apollo and Diana in fact killed his children with arrows launched from the sky. The so-called Medici vase, a neo-Attic crater from the 1st Century BC, also comes from Villa Medici.

CARAVAGGIO
Bacchus
Dated to between 1596
and 1600

The painting can be attributed to Caravaggio's early days, when he worked for Cardinal Francesco Maria Del Monte, who donated this work, as well as the *Medusa*, to Ferdinando de' Medici. The painter, interpreting the mythological theme in a strictly realistic fashion, portrays *Bacchus*, the Greek god, not only of wine and intemperance, but also of fertility, as symbolised in the painting by the splendid white faience fruit bowl replete with autumn fruit. The youth, dressed according to the ancient manner, seems to hold up the wine goblet in offering. For centuries, Bacchus' features were thought to represent a self-portrait of the artist. More recently, however, the portrait has been identified as that of the Sicilian painter Mario Minniti, who lived for a time with Caravaggio in Rome. The elements of raw representation of the 'real', such as the colour variations of the skin, the puffy mouth, dirty fingernails (poorly befitting a divinity) and bruised or rotten fruit, testify to the nature of Caravaggio's realism. Like all his northern contemporaries who travelled to Rome, he was attracted by the charm of the classical world, while at the same time, bound to the empirical, acute observation and representation of reality bequeathed to him by the painting of 16th-century Brescia.

CARAVAGGIO
Sacrifice of Isaac
Dated to between 1592 and 1604

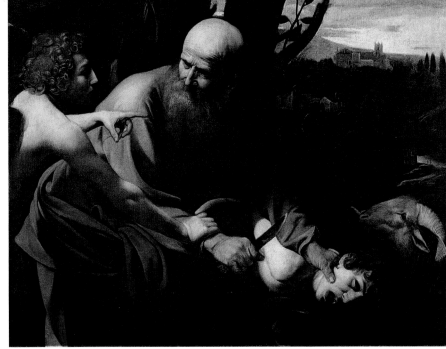

The work, whose date of execution is uncertain, was probably carried out for Cardinal Maffeo Barberini, the future Pope Urban VIII. Donated to the Uffizi by John Fairfax Murray in 1917, the canvas depicts the biblical episode in which Abraham, in the act of sacrificing his son at God's bidding, is stopped by an angel. Caravaggio displaces the angel's act so it takes place, not in the heavens, as described in the sacred texts, but at Abraham's side where he stays the determined father's hand by firmly grabbing his wrist. Together with Isaac's desperate cry, this accentuates the scene's realism and, through its physicality, expresses the peak of dramatic representation. On the right appears the ram sent by God to take Isaac's place in the sacrifice. A serene landscape reminiscent of Venetian painting serves as backdrop, in stark contrast with the scene's dynamism.

CARAVAGGIO
Medusa
Dated to between 1592 and 1600

It was Cardinal Francesco Maria del Monte, the Tuscan grand duke's representative to the papal Curia, who sent this tournament shield, painted by Caravaggio during the last decade of the 16th Century, to Ferdinando de' Medici. Upon its arrival in Florence it was destined for the Uffizi Armoury, where it was to accompany an armoured oriental horseman (now lost) seated on a wooden horse in the centre of the first hall. At the Medici court there was a da Vinci painting of the *Medusa* that must have influenced Caravaggio, as did the scientific illustrations of Jacopo Ligozzi. The strangled cry issuing from the wide-open mouth, and the fixity of her gaze admirably accomplish the artist's design of rendering the scene horrifying. Though convex, the work's perspective and the shadows cast by the serpents make the wood-backed canvas appear concave.

31

Located in what were once the buildings of the monastery of San Matteo and convent of San Niccolò di Cafaggio, the Galleria della Accademia was established in 1784 by the grand duke of Tuscany, Pietro Leopoldo, so that the students at the adjoining Accademia delle Belle Arti (Fine Arts Academy) could practice on renowned examples of ancient art. With the suppression of religious establishments in 1785 and 1808, the original core collection, acquired for the most part by the Medici, was expanded upon. In 1873, the arrival of Michelangelo's *David*, moved from its original site outside Palazzo della Signoria (p. 126) mostly for its preservation, prompted the building of the apse or Tribuna, completed by the architect de Fabris in 1882. Since then the fame of the Gallery has been inextricably linked to this statue, arguably the world's best-known sculpture, which together with the other works by Michelangelo – the *Prisoners* (or *Slaves*), *Saint Matthew* and the *Palestrina Pietà* – makes up an extraordinary harmonious whole. The 19th-century Room now houses a collection of plaster casts by Lorenzo Bartolini and Luigi Pampaloni, two early 19th-century Tuscan sculptors. Also on exhibit here is an extraordinary collection of paintings providing a comprehensive panorama of Tuscan painting from the late 13th Century up to the end of 14th Century and important paintings from the 15th and 16th Centuries. The singular collection of Russian icons once belonged to the Lorraine grand dukes. Finally, the musical instruments now exhibited in the "Room of the Colossus" are destined for a separate new museum, associated to the Gallery, to be hosted in rooms of the adjoining State Conservatory "Luigi Cherubini".

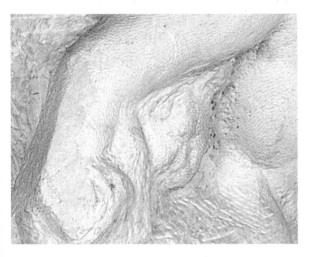

MICHELANGELO BUONARROTI

Prisoners
circa 1530
Gallery of the Slaves

The first prisoner, the *Young slave*, is shown bent-kneed, burdened by fatigue in the act of raising his arm above his head, the sculptural anatomy exhibiting different degrees of finish. The second, *Reawakening slave*, emerges painstakingly from the depths of sleep, just as

Page 32:
Michelangelo Buonarroti,
Prisoner *Atlas* and *David*,
Page 33:
Prisoner *Young slave*

Below at left:
Prisoner *Reawakening slave*
Below at right:
Prisoner *Bearded slave*

his figure emerges from the marble block enveloping it. We then come to the prisoner called the *Bearded slave*, the most complete of the three, whose sculpted anatomy interplays softly with the impinging light in plastic clarity. Finally, there is the one known as *Atlas*, straining in his effort to uphold an enormous rock from which his head, still imprisoned in stone, has not yet been completely unloosed. These are extraordinary examples of Michelangelo's "unfinished" work: though in different states of completion, the sculptures convey the Herculean effort needed to release the subject from the material imprisoning it, almost as if to symbolise the strivings of man to free himself of sin. This is the key to the most accredited (and suggestive) reading of these works, destined for the tomb of Pope Julius II della Rovere, though never used (just as the Louvre *Slaves* and *Victory* in Palazzo Vecchio), and which the artist's nephew donated to Cosimo I, who had them set in the Buontalenti Grotto in Boboli Gardens, where they remained up to 1909.

MICHELANGELO
BUONARROTI

Saint Matthew
1505-1506
Gallery of the Slaves

In April 1503 the Wool Guild and Cathedral Workers charged Michelangelo with the task of sculpting the twelve apostles for the pillars of the Florentine Duomo. The artist was to deliver the statues at the rate of one a year, but because of commitments made to Pope Julius II in Rome, the contract was never fulfilled, and the statues were later commissioned from other sculptors. The only one remaining is the unfinished *Saint Matthew*, which reveals how Michelangelo proceeded, "by way of raising", to make the figure issue forth from the marble block. It can in fact be noticed that the left leg is in a state of greater completion than the rest of the body, still engulfed in stone, though the twisting of the torso gives rise to a dramatic sense of tension.

MICHELANGELO
BUONARROTI

Palestrina Pietà
circa 1560
Gallery of the Slaves

This *Pietà* originally came from the Barberini chapel in the church of Santa Rosalia in Palestrina (hence its name). It was executed on marble taken from Roman ruins, though little else is known about it as no documentary evidence exists. Christ's disproportionately large torso and right arm serve to accentuate the heavy look of his body as it is upheld by Mary's hand, with which its merges. Altthough Michelangel's authorship has been placed in doubt by some who would ascribe it instead to one of his followers, the compositional concept, as well as formal elements argue for its having been executed by the maestro himself.

MICHELANGELO BUONARROTI
David
1501-1504
Tribuna

In 1501 the Cathedral Workers of Florence entrusted Michelangelo with the sculpting of David, the biblical vanquisher of Goliath. The block of marble had already been worked in the late 15th Century and abandoned immediately due to technical difficulties, mostly because of its veining. Michelangelo instead accepted the challenge and in three years brought to completion a work of such dimensions that it caused great consternation for the difficulty of transporting it along the narrow city streets. At the end of long debate, a committee of artists, including Leonardo da Vinci, decided to place the work on the communal pulpit before the façade of Palazzo della Signoria. This was indeed the place best befitting the significance that the citizens of the Florentine Republic immediately attributed to the sculpture: a symbol of civil virtue and an admonition to the enemies of liberty. The sculptor choose to depict him as a classical hero, completely naked, with proud confident gaze turned towards the enemy, Goliath (whose head had up to that time always been represented at David's feet); one hand cradling the stone, while the other wields the sling, captured in the instant just before the fateful act. The disproportionately large head and hands, which detract not the least from the beauty of the heroic figure, were portrayed so on purpose, to convey a precise moral: to underscore man's dual nature, made up, respectively of Thought and Action. Since 1873 the colossal masterpiece has been kept in the Accademia Gallery, where the Tribuna was built specifically to host it.

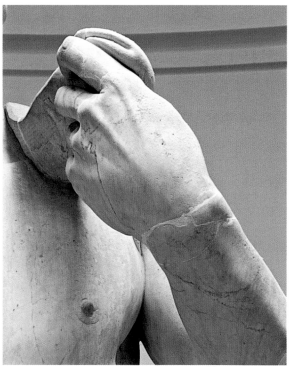

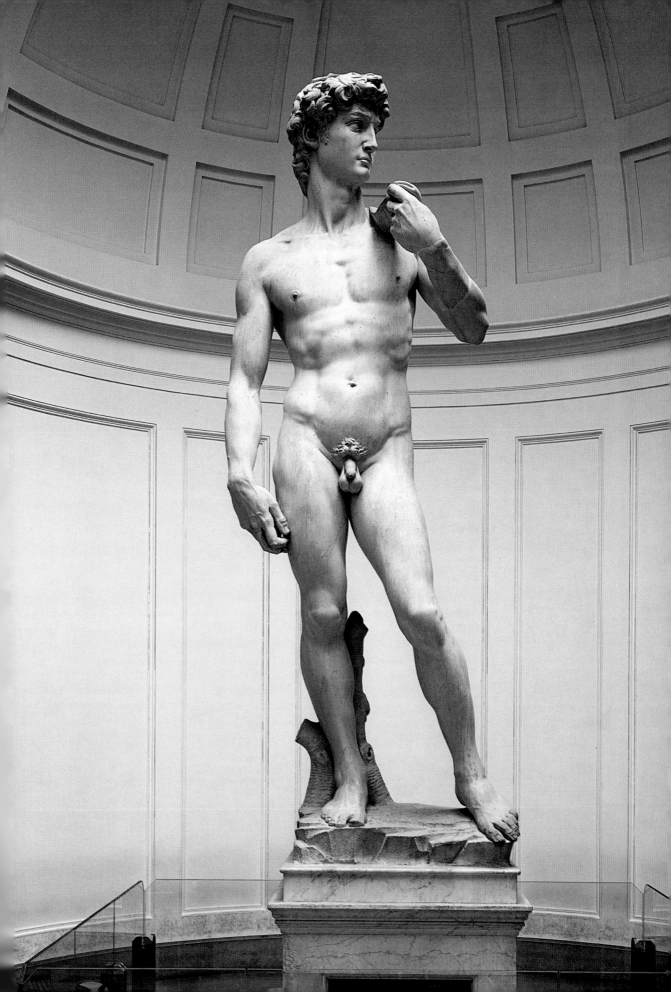

PAOLO UCCELLO

Scenes from monastic life ("Tebaide")
circa 1460
Florentine Rooms

The canvas, cut on all four sides, comes from the Monastery of San Giorgio alla Costa, even if its likely original setting was inside the adjoining convent of San Girolamo and San Francesco alla Costa, a fact argued for by the presence of these saints in the painting. The work illustrates episodes of coenobitic life, set in a countryside where the grottoes and tree canopy serve a perspective function and isolate the single scenes: *Saint Benedict Preaching*, *The Appearance of the Virgin to Saint Bernard*, *Saint Jerome Worshipping the Crucifix* and *The Stigmata of Saint Francis*, in order of perspective priority that seems to indicate the order in which it is to be read. The fact that different religious orders are mixed together is justified by the painting's subject: an ideal path through the way to perfection, inspired by an 13th-century treatise that stressed the importance of contemplation in attaining knowledge of the divine. Despite the many hypotheses advanced regarding the picture's creator, by now Paolo Uccello's authorship seems undisputed because of its affinities with other works by the mature painter.

LO SCHEGGIA

Dance scene ("Cassone Adimari")
circa 1450
Florentine Rooms

This panel was once thought to be the front piece of a large chest (cassone) painted with scenes of the festivities that took place on the occasion of the wedding of Boccaccio Adimari and Lisa Ricasoli on June 22, 1420. Now, as a recent study has revealed, it is instead thought to be part of one of the wooden panels used during the Renaissance to adorn the walls of homes as isolation from the cold and damp. Giovanni di ser Giovanni, known as "Lo Scheggia", to whom the painting has been attributed, was Masaccio's younger brother and an expert in this kind of profane painting for residential interior decoration. It was painted between the 1450s and 1460s, as revealed by stylistic considerations and manner of dress. It is precisely these, together with the meticulous rendition of the architecture, that represent this work's appeal. In the square closed in by Renaissance and medieval buildings, amongst which the Florentine Baptistery looms large, a dance is unfolding: five courtly young couples dance sheltered from the sun under a canvas tent, while the musicians of the Signoria play on stage.

DOMENICO GHIRLANDAIO

Saint Stephen between Saints James and Peter
1493
Florentine Rooms

This pala, or altarpiece, was commissioned by Stefano di Jacopo Boni for the family altar in the church of Santa Maria Maddalena de' Pazzi. According to ancient sources, the original figure of Saint Stephen was repainted as Saint Jerome by Fra Bartolomeo in 1513, a modification undone only in the 19th Century. The figures of Saints James, Stephen and Peter are very similar in composition to the painting on the high altar of Saint Maria Novella, performed by Ghirlandaio in those same years.

SANDRO BOTTICELLI

Virgin and Child with young Saint John and two angels
circa 1468
Florentine Rooms

Originally from the hospital of Santa Maria Nuova, the panel is attributed to Botticelli in his early years, when having just finished his apprenticeship with Filippo Lippi (1464-1467), he was working in the workshop of Verrocchio. The painting follows a wide-spread compositional scheme with numerous variations found as well in plaster works of private religious worship.

FILIPPINO LIPPI AND PERUGINO
Deposition
1504 and 1507
Room of the Colossus

This painting, together with others, including Perugino's *Assumption* (Santissima Annunziata, fifth chapel to the left), was part of a complex decoration destined for the main altar of the church of Santissima Annunziata. In 1503 the Servites commissioned the work to Filippino Lippi, who died only a few months later, leaving completed only the painting's upper portion, still lacking Christ's body. The crowd of characters in precarious equilibrium on the staircase, and the elegant arabesques of the ribbons underscore the stylistic key of Lippi's art. The work was then entrusted to Perugino, who completed it by 1507: the group of mourners show the peaceful tones and serene equilibrium of this master from Umbria.

PONTORMO
Venus and Cupid
circa 1535
Right wing of the Tribuna

This work testifies to the friendship and artistic bond between Michelangelo and Pontormo: the former provided the cartoon that was translated into painting by the latter. Michelangelo's design is evident in the plastic nudity of Venus and Cupid, inserted into a landscape revealing the personality of Pontormo. It was destined for the nuptial chamber of Bartolomeo Bettini, but was acquired by Alessandro de' Medici, much to the disappointment of Michelangelo, who at the time harboured no great liking for the tyrannical duke.

PACINO DI BUONAGUIDA
Tree of Life
1305-1310
13th and early 14th-century Room

In 1274 Bonaventura da Bagnoregio, saint of the Franciscan order, wrote a poetic composition entitled *Lignum Vitae*. Pacino di Buonaguida took inspiration from this to tackle the theme so dear to the Franciscan order, the Cross of Christ. In fact the panel, which comes from the Clarisse convent in Monticelli, depicts Christ on the cross on Mount Golgotha: from the cross stem twelve branches with circular illustrations of his life. The vivid colours and freshness of detail reveal the art of this painter, formed on Giotto's early work, and also a skilled illuminator. The work therefore manifests itself as a sacred text whose immediate visual impact aims to attract as well as to enlighten. The theme of the *Tree of Life* would be taken up again around 1345 by Taddeo Gaddi, who would render it monumentally in his frescoed version in the refectory of the convent of Santa Croce (p. 60).

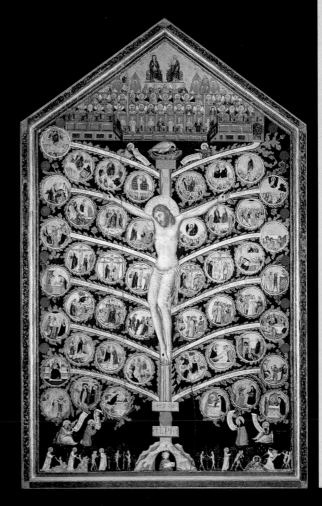

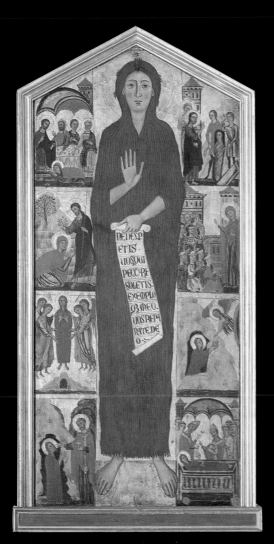

MAESTRO DELLA MADDALENA
Penitent Mary Magdalene and eight scenes from her life
circa 1280-1285
13th and early 14th-century Room

This anonymous master, named precisely for this panel carried out in his later years, was active in a Florentine shop attentive to the innovations introduced by Cimabue. Its original site was the convent of Santissima Annunziata. The painter represents the hieratic figure of Mary Magdalene in a frontal position, following a compositional style more common in thirteenth-century altarpieces (see, for example, the altarpiece with San Francis in the Bardi Chapel at Santa Croce (p. 157). Magdalene is covered only by her hair, according to an already widespread iconographic formula, and flanked by stories from her life portrayed didactically. Despite their small dimensions, the scenes, with hints of a landscape, possess a narrative vivacity that Giotto would develop to new heights in the following years.

TADDEO GADDI
Scenes from the life of Christ and Saint Francis
circa 1333
Giottesque Rooms

The two lunettes, together with the twenty-two panels (four more are currently found in Berlin and Munich), come from the sacristy of Santa Croce. They originally decorated wooden furnishings, perhaps reliquaries, such as the two in Santa Croce holding a thorn of Christ's crown and a fragment of the True Cross; some may have come from a "manganella", a type of folding bench. Within the mixtilinear frames, which recall the style already adopted by Andrea Pisano for the panels of the Baptistery door, Taddeo Gaddi illustrates the lives of Christ and Saint Francis in parallel, according to an iconographic theme very dear to the Franciscan order. The figures' solid volumes and architecture's perspective reveal his perfect understanding of the teachings of Giotto, of whom he was a devoted follower. This is not the only important commission that the painter carried out for Santa Croce: in fact, he decorated the Baroncelli chapel just prior to beginning these panels and, in the late sixties, did the monumental fresco in the refectory (p. 60) and the *Crucifixion* in the sacristy.

BERNARDO DADDI
Crucifix
circa 1348
Giottesque Rooms

Bernardo Daddi had assimilated the lessons of Giotto by the time he painted this large Crucifix, which probably hung above the main altar of the Church of San Donato in Polverosa, whence it originates. Side by side are the full figures of Christ, Saint Mary and Saint John, while scenes from the Passion of Christ are depicted on the extremities of the cross.

GIOVANNI DA MILANO
Christ in Pietà
1365
Room of Giovanni da Milano

This cusped panel, from the convent of San Girolamo and San Francesco alla Costa, is the only dated work by Giovanni da Milano, as can be read in the inscription amongst the coats of arms of Strozzi and Rinieri, who commissioned the work. The painter, originally from a village near Como, took on the name 'da Milano' and signed his paintings as such to give the idea that he was from Milan, for obvious reasons of prestige. Though Lombard by training, his work was carried out primarily in Tuscany. The frescoes of the Guidalotti-Rinuccini chapel in the sacristy of Santa Croce are from the same period as *Christ in Pietà* – an important testimony to artistic developments after Giotto, which reveal how Giovanni da Milano supplemented the naturalism and attention to detail typical of the northern tradition with a Giottesque study of plasticity. These are the same elements that can also be appreciated in the *Pietà*, dramatically constrained within the restricted space of the panel.

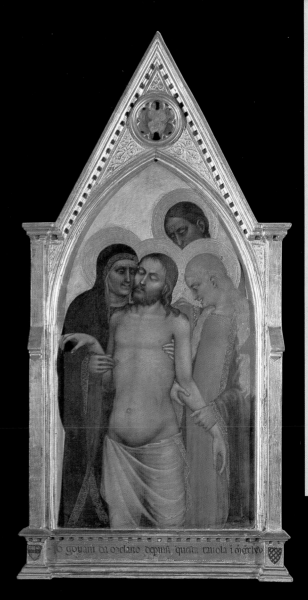

LORENZO MONACO
Oration in the garden
circa 1395
Room of Lorenzo Monaco

Lorenzo Monaco belonged to the Camaldolite order and lived in the convent of Santa Maria degli Angeli, where a school of illuminators flourished - an art at which Monaco excelled. This panel originates from the convent and is to be counted amongst the artist's earliest work, well rooted in the Florentine tradition, with clear references to the painting of Giotto, as the two apostles in the foreground reveal.

43

NATIONAL ARCHAEOLOGY MUSEUM

The Palazzo della Crocetta, built in 1619-1620 by Giulio Parigi for Maria Maddalena de' Medici, has housed the Florentine National Archaeology Museum since 1881. Thanks to the efforts of its first curator, Luigi Adriano Milani, its rooms boast a vast compendium of artwork, including the outstanding collection of masterpieces of Etruscan art, fundamental to the study and understanding of this ancient civilisation. Amongst these is the famous *Chimera* found in Arezzo in 1553, the bronze statue of the *Haranguer,* as well as numerous cinerary urns. The important Egyptian Collection, Italy's second largest after the Egyptian Museum in Turin, is made up of the splendid archaeological finds that came to the museum above all thanks to 19th-century archaeological expeditions. The collection of ancient ceramics alone would deserve a separate visit. Noteworthy amongst these are the celebrated *François Vase* and the two, uniquely fascinating *kouroi* known as the *Milani Apollo* and *Apollino*, the only existing examples of original Greek archaics in Italy.

Statue of Ptahmose
New Kingdom, 13th Dynasty, Reign of Amenoph III (1413-1377 BC)
First floor, Room III

The grey granite statue depicts Ptahmose, an Egyptian dignitary who lived during the reign of Amenoph III. Apart from the inscription on the right shoulder that bears an engraving of the Pharaoh's first name, corroboration of this dating also comes from the complexity of the wig and the finely pleated dress, elements that testify to the luxury and refined customs prevailing during the reign of Amenoph III, when Egypt enjoyed a period of domestic security and dominion over its foreign territories. Typical of this epoch is also the delicate expression on the face of Ptahmose, who holds a stand on which a now lost figurine of a deity must have rested. As indicated by the inscription painted on the back, the statue was sculpted at the request of Ptahmose's son, Kay, and dedicated to his father.

Cartonnage covering for Takerheb
Ptolemaic Epoch (304-30 BC)
First floor, Room VIII

The mummy of Takerheb, a young girl who lived during the Ptolemaic dynasty, is not contained in a true sarcophagus, but in a wrap made through a procedure called *cartonnage*, documented as far back as the third intermediate period, around 900 BC. The method consisted of applying various layers of cloth directly onto the mummy, which was then plastered and decorated. The rich decoration of the wrap shows, amongst the numerous figures of deities, also the scene of the mummification of the body lying on a funeral bed, carried out by the jackal-headed god Anubis. Under the bed one can see the vases in which the viscera removed from the dead were placed, together with the brain, during the mummification procedure. The wrap is embellished by the application of thin golden foil, used in the face and neck area, as well as in the representation of several divinities. The mummy, which was sectioned in 1827, is visible beneath the wrap. The true sarcophagus, made of wood, is on display in the adjacent showcase.

Chimera
Late 5th - early 4th Century BC
First floor, Room XIV

The sculpture represents the mythical three-headed creature (lion, goat and serpent) with lion's body, *Chimera*, already wounded, in its valiant and vain attempt to defend itself from the attack of the Greek hero, Bellerophon astride the winged horse, Pegasus. Judging by the inscription on the front right leg, the sculpture was probably one of a votive sculptural group that also included a statue of Bellerophon. Originally from northern Etruria, the bronze has been dated to the end of the 5th – beginnings of the 4th Century BC, while the tail is the result of an eighteenth-century restoration. Traditionally, the left legs were attributed to Benvenuto Cellini, a hypothesis that must be dismissed as no more than legend. The realistic rendering of the beast's anatomy is evident as it apprehensively tenses to avoid the arrows shot by the hero. Discovered in 1553 in Arezzo, the statue was immediately added to the grand duke's collections. In fact, at the time Cosimo I, an avid collector of Etruscan works, was looking to justify his expansionistic designs by exalting Tuscany's Etruscan heritage.

"Haranguer"
Early 1st Century BC
First floor, Room XIV

The bronze statue, discovered in 1566, represents the Etruscan nobleman, Aulo Metello, in the act of calling the assembly to silence in order to give his speech. The nobleman, portrayed in maturity, wears a tunic, a short toga and footwear, articles of clothing that attest to the by then complete Romanisation of Etruria, even if the work, which dates back to the beginnings of the first century BC, must surely be counted amongst Etruscan art. Such origins are attested to by a number of facts, including the inscription dedicating the statue is to the god Tece Sans, a deity revered in the lake Trasimeno area where the statue was found. After an eventful history, the celebrated statue was finally acquired by Cosimo I de' Medici.

ERGÒTIMOS AND KLEITÌAS

François Vase
570 BC
Second floor, Room I, showcase 4

This monumental Attic crater gets its name from Alessandro François, who discovered it near Chiusi in 1844. It is an admirable, extremely refined example of Attica vase art from the age of Pisistratos. Work of the potter Ergòtimos and the ceramics painter Kleitìas, it arrived in Italy as a gift for an Etruscan lord. The rich decoration, in which a host of mythological characters is represented, was masterfully executed by Kleitìas along a series of superimposed bands, in a work giving vent to both his penchant for narration and his great pictorial ability. The central episode, along the vase's widest part, represents the solemn *Procession of divinities for the wedding of Thetis and Peleus*, Achilles' parents. No precise narrative design appears discernible, though events linked to Achilles seem to be given particular emphasis. The vase was executed in the black-figure technique, which consisted of embellishing the black-painted background figures with touches of red or white paint and finishing the figures' inner details through graffito (i.e., incising with a fine instrument). Such a technique allowed for a wide range of pictorial solutions.

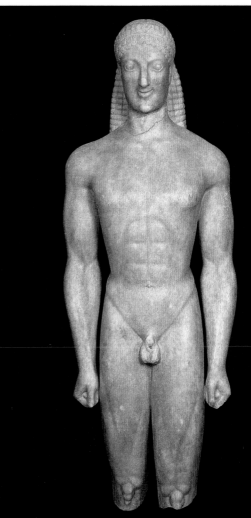

Statue of kouros ("Milani Apollo")
530 BC
Second floor, sculpture corridor

This splendid *kouros* (as are known such nude masculine figures from the archaic age around the 6th Century BC) is a rare example of an Attic original of unknown origin, dating back to 530 BC. Together with the other sculpture known as the *Milani Apollino* (young Apollo), acquired at the same time by Luigi Adriano Milani for the museum, it represents the only example in Italy of a Greek original from the archaic age. Typical of the works of this period is the so-called "archaic smile" which, rather than constituting a pictorial feature, is instead a technical expedient used to overcome frontality by raising the corners of the mouth, so as to suggest depth. The figure is sculpted according to a solid scanning of well-delineated, sharply contoured planes, while the muscles are represented through incisions and furrows. The face, despite the evident restoration of the nose and chin, conserves its original quality of vivacious expressiveness.

Idolino
First Century AD
Ground floor

The bronze statue, representing a young, slightly muscled boy, has always been known as the *Idolino* (young idol), almost in testimony to the ephebic grace of the subject. Until recently the sculpture, following the style of the sculptor Polycletus, was considered to be one of the most fascinating representatives of Greek originals handed down from antiquity. Instead, it has been recognised as originating from the Augustan age, that is to say, it is an example of the fine artwork, fashioned after classical models, that adorned the homes of the Roman aristocracy. In particular, the *Idolino* performed the function of lamp holder for illuminating night-time banquets. In fact, the left hand once held a vine shoot, detached during a 17th-century restoration because it was considered to be irrelevant. The sculpture was discovered in Pesaro in 1530 and reached Florence as a gift from Francesco II Maria della Rovere to his niece, Vittoria for her engagement to the grand duke of Tuscany, Ferdinando II. The sixteenth-century base, inspired by the Roman *arae* and sculpted by Girolamo Lombardo, bears an inscription composed by the renaissance poet Pietro Bembo alluding to the cult of Dionysus, as the youth had been identified as.

BARDINI MUSEUM

In 1881 Stefano Bardini (1836-1922), collector and antiquary of international fame, acquired and transformed the thirteenth-century convent complex of San Gregorio in Pace according to the eclectic style then in fashion, reutilising architectural and decorative elements from different epochs. The building and the collection it housed were donated by the express will of Bardini to the Municipality of Florence upon his death in 1922. There are paintings and sculptures, majolicas and weapons, musical instruments, furniture and stonework, carpets and tapestries to testify to the extraordinary collection that Bardini accumulated here, as well as in his other places of residence, aided by his uncommon gift of discernment and the particular situation in Italy during the late 19th Century. The museum also holds the valuable collection of paintings from varying periods donated by Fortunata Carobbi Corsi in 1937.

TINO DI CAMAINO
Charity
circa 1321
Rooms VII-VIII

We do not know the origins of this female figure in the caring, motherly act of nursing two seemingly sprightly infants – the very personification of the Theological Virtue of *Charity*. However, it must have been placed so as to be viewed from below, and was therefore probably set in a niche, perhaps inside a more extensive funeral monument. Influenced by Arnolfo di Cambio, the vigorous and synthetic plasticity of this group appears in strict relation to the statue of Bishop Orso in the funeral monument erected by Tino di Camaino on the western wall of Santa Maria del Fiore. The sculptor from Siena reached Florence in 1318 and remained there until he was called to the Angevin court in Naples.

49

DONATELLO

Virgin and Child with angels ("Madonna dei cordai")
Door panels 1443
Room XIV

This bas-relief reveals Donatello's experimentalism: in order to simulate a mosaic background, he covered the panel with gilded leather tessera covered with glass. By now, the mosaic pieces have largely fallen off, and the figures of the four angels have also been lost. In fact, the preparatory sketch traced out on the wood of the panel are visible. Over this, the artist modelled the plaster figures which were subsequently painted by an unknown artist. The Madonna, sitting on a faldstool, holds the Child Jesus on her lap and amuses him with some twine; while the angels play with wooden disks called "ruzzole".

ANTONIO DEL
POLLAIOLO

*Saint Michael the
Archangel and the dragon*
circa 1465
Room XVIII

This is the back of the standard that Antonio del Pollaiolo painted before 1465 for the Compagnia di Sant' Arcangelo of Arezzo. The position of Saint Michael the Archangel is analogous to that in the panel, currently in the Uffizi, depicting *Hercules and the Hydra*, thus daringly transposing the pagan theme of the Greek hero, often present in the artist's work, to a painting of religious significance. The figure of the archangel stands out imposingly from the background landscape in colours typical of Pollaiolo, in which all appears to be made smaller by the distance. Despite the figure's power, its gesture appears rather rigid – so much so that a collaboration between Antonio and his brother Pietro has been speculated (if not the sole authorship of the latter). The stylistic reading of the painting has surely been influenced by the numerous restorative operations carried out on it over the centuries.

MUSEO DELL'OPERA DEL DUOMO

The museum is located in the building that Brunelleschi restructured in the early 15th Century when l'Opera del Duomo (i.e., Cathedral Works) was transferred there. Since the late 13th Century the Magistratura was assigned to supervising the construction of the new cathedral, which in 1331 was placed under the patronage of the Wool Guild, whose symbol, the *Agnus Dei*, is found throughout the buildings. Works destined for the cathedral or those removed because of changing tastes were temporarily housed in these quarters. Only in 1885 was it instituted as a true museum that was inaugurated in 1891 as soon as the site had been restored. Here, works from the Cathedral, Baptistery and Bell Tower, as well as many pieces recovered from other religious buildings, have been gathered to form an extraordinary collection of sculptures, liturgical paraments and masterpieces of jewellery that illustrate the artistic vicissitudes of the most renowned monuments of the city.

ARNOLFO DI CAMBIO
Madonna and Child
1296
Room of the ancient Façade

Arnolfo di Cambio, the architect that designed the new cathedral of Santa Maria del Fiore, also oversaw, together with his thriving workshop, the sculptural decoration of the façade, demolished in 1587 by will of grand duke Ferdinando I. The *Madonna and Child* occupied the lunette of the central portal, flanked by *Saint Reparata and Saint Zanobius*. From afar it must have appeared vibrant due to the by now lost colours that partly covered it, as well as the unusual glass eyes. Even though it preserves a Byzantine-like fixity, it nevertheless manifests a fullness of form and volume rendered with a plastic clarity approaching even the works of Giotto.

NANNI DI BANCO

Saint Luke the Evangelist

1408-1414

DONATELLO

*Saint John
the Evangelist*

1408-1415
Room of the
ancient Façade

The building of the cathedral of Santa Maria del Fiore represented a great challenge for the main Florentine sculptors of the early 15th Century who were to sculpt the figures of the four Evangelists for the niches on either side of the central portal, according to the original project by Arnolfo di Cambio. With the statues of *St. Luke* and *Saint John the Evangelist*, Nanni di Banco and Donatello clearly go beyond the gothic formulation that still prevailed in Niccolò di Pietro Lamberti's *Saint Mark* and Bernardo Ciuffagni's *Saint Mathew*. While Nanni di Banco more strictly adheres to the classical ideal, nobly sculpting a harmonious figure, Donatello draws upon ancient sculpture as inspiration for his search to adhere to reality – a psychological reality – and fashions a frowning figure whose limbs wave with trembling vitality below his richly draping robes.

Above:
Donatello, *Saint John the Evangelist*

At left:
Nanni di Banco, *Saint Luke the Evangelist* 53

MICHELANGELO BUONARROTI
Pietà
1550-1555
Mezzanine

With this *Pietà*, Michelangelo returns to the theme he had addressed so many years earlier for Saint Peter's Basilica, giving it a pyramidal scheme similar to that masterpiece. According to the artist's biographers, Michelangelo began this work for his own tomb, which he had planned for Saint Maria Maggiore in Rome. The group was probably greatly influenced by Michelangelo's reflections on death, as he was now well on in years and upset by the disappearance of his close friend Vittoria Colonna. The work was never completed; rather, Michelangelo attempted to destroy it. It was subsequently acquired by the Florentine sculptor Francesco Bandini, who entrusted its restoration to a student of Michelangelo, Tiberio Calcagni, who recalling the maestro's sketches, completed the figure of Mary Magdalene and Christ's leg. The group remained for a long time in the garden of Bandini's Roman residence and then finally reached Florence in 1674 when it was acquired by the grand duke Cosimo III. The work clearly reveals the religious torment of the artist, whose portrait Vasari discerned in the figure of the old man, perhaps Nicodemus, looming over the other figures. Its "unfinishedness" surely accents the dramatic atmosphere of the group, which despite being spurned by its creator, remains a fascinating testimony to his utmost art.

Luca della Robbia

Cantoria
1431-1438
Choir room, left wall

Donatello

Cantoria
1433-1439
Choir room, right wall

The *Cantoria* (Choir) by Luca della Robbia, originally located above the door of the Sacristy of Masses, held the new main organ of Santa Maria del Fiore. Just opposite and symmetrical to this, above the portal of the Sacristy of Canons, Donatello's marble balcony choir bore the restored old organ. The *Cantorie* were partly removed in 1688, and definitively dismantled during the 19th Century. Their restoration has required some portions to be replaced and added, and since 1889 they have been kept in the Museo dell'Opera del Duomo. The pulpit by Luca della Robbia is composed of ten reliefs on two levels where children can be seen playing, dancing and singing in illustration of the verses of *Psalm 150*, inscribed on the frames. Classical in style, its peaceful figures are modelled after Roman sarcophagi and Greek medallions. Donatello instead looks to a different antiquity, favouring a Dionysian tone in the dance of the angels that unfolds uninterrupted over a bed of leaves, on a mosaic background created with small 'tessere' of coloured glass. The two *Cantorie* appear as musical interpretations of the diverse rhythms of two Psalms (or different parts of the same Psalm), according to a grand design perhaps conceived of by Brunelleschi, at the time engaged in completing the cathedral cupola.

DONATELLO
Jeremiah and Habakkuk ("Lo Zuccone")
1426-1432
Choir Room

The two prophets Jeremiah and Habakkuk make up part of the group of sixteen statues that decorated the niches of the bell tower of the Florentine cathedral. They were executed at different times by Andrea Pisano, Nanni di Bartolo and, of course, Donatello. In these two sculptures the artist unites careful study of reality with his wide knowledge of Roman portraiture, attaining extraordinary results in representing the characters' physiognomies. So much so that, beginning with Vasari, an old tradition has it that they represent portraits of two of the artist's contemporaries. It is life that animates the facial expressions and slender limbs of the two prophets: one is so thoroughly bald that he has been dubbed "lo Zuccone" (squash-head), the other, frowning with pursed lips. The statues are designed to be viewed from below at a great distance, and nonetheless Donatello infuses them with the breath of life. His rendering of the robes, especially in Jeremiah, abandon the linearity of the classical toga to fuse in a complex and articulated play of folds, as if the wind were modelling them over the prophets' bodies.

FLORENTINE MASTERS
Altar-frontal of St. John
1366-1480
Altar room

The precious altar-frontal in gilded and enamelled silver was originally to protect and embellish the Baptistery altar. Commissioned by the Calimala Guild, patron of the building, it is the result of the combined efforts of some of Florence's greatest goldsmiths and sculptors over the period from 1366 to 1480, when Andrea del Verrocchio and Antonio del Pollaiolo, together with other artists, completed it by adding the lateral reliefs. The elegant statuette of *Saint John the Baptist* in the central niche is the work of Michelozzo. This is flanked by reliefs with *Stories of the Saint* and framed by gothic niches with figurines set on the crowning and pillars, inspired by the ornamentation of the cathedral's southern portal and the bell tower by Giotto. The *Cross* surmounting the altar is a collaborative work by many artists – amongst whom, Antonio del Pollaiolo deserves special mention. It serves as reliquary for a fragment of the Cross that arrived here from Constantinople in 1459.

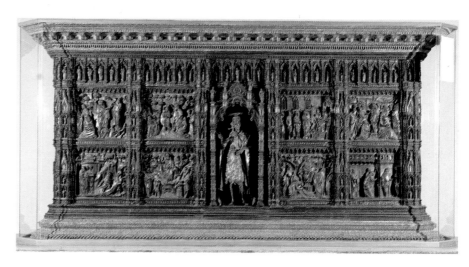

This dramatic, realistic representation of *Mary Magdalene* as an old woman, consumed by the fast and abstinence of her penitence in the desert, with hands seeming to join in prayer without however touching, and emaciated aspect exalted by the wood, conveys a sense of profound spirituality. Identification of the by now elderly sculptor with the theme of his work follows almost spontaneously: it is his reflection on old age and the salvation one must attain by renouncing all worldly temptations. Sculpted around the mid 1450s, the work has been set in relation to the illness that afflicted the sculptor in those years, when he returned to Florence after a stay in Padua, also prompted by renewed interest on the part of the Medici for his art. Prior to its current location, *Mary Magdalene* was found in the Baptistery, where it has been documented from 1500.

"La porta del Paradiso" (door to Heaven) was Michelangelo's definition. This world-renowned masterpiece was the last door of the Florentine Baptistery to be executed. The oldest is that on the southern side, signed by Andrea Pisano in 1330. Then, in 1401, the Calimala Guild, patron of the Baptistery, announced a competition for the second, northern door. The coveted right to perform the work fell to the sculptor and goldsmith, Lorenzo Ghiberti. As the results attained more than lived up to expectations, in 1425 he was entrusted with carrying out the third door, set in place in 1452 at the Baptistery's most important point, the side facing the cathedral. To narrate the *Stories of the Old Testament*, from *Adam and Eve* to the *Meeting of Solomon with the Queen of Sheba*, Ghiberti reduced the number of panels, initially planned according to an iconographic design suggested by the humanist Leonardo Bruni, and abandoned the mixtilinear frames in favour of ten square panels in gilded bronze. This allowed him to fit more episodes inside each single tile in a complex spatial design rendered according to the then new rules of perspective and through the use of different degrees of relief. The original door panels have been replaced with copies and are now preserved in the museum.

DONATELLO
Mary Magdalene
circa 1455
Altar room

LORENZO GHIBERTI AND COLLABORATORS
Scenes from the Old Testament
1425-1452
Old courtyard

Lorenzo Ghiberti, *Stories of Adam and Eve*   Lorenzo Ghiberti, *Stories of Cain and Abel*   Lorenzo Ghiberti, *Stories of Joseph*

MUSEO DELL'OPERA DI SANTA CROCE

The museum, which is housed in what was once a Franciscan convent, looks out upon the first cloister in the complex, delimited to the left by a portico-covered gallery of 19th-century funeral monuments from abroad. Also leading onto the cloister is the Pazzi Chapel, a consummate example of Brunelleschi's architecture. Despite numerous alterations, the cloister itself preserves its original fourteenth-century air. The flood of November 4th 1966 struck these sites mercilessly, seriously damaging Taddeo Gaddi's fresco of the *Last Supper* and Cimabue's *Crucifix*, both on the back wall of the large refectory. The adjoining minor refectory bears a fresco by Jacopo Ligozzi and fragments of the original glass doors from the Basilica. In the centre of the next room (formerly the Cerchi family Chapel) stands the reliquary bust of the beatified Umiliana dei Cerchi. Crossing the next rooms containing, amongst other works, the funeral monument to Gastone della Torre by Tino di Camaino, and exiting through the doorway by Benedetto da Maiano, one comes to the second cloister, completed in 1453, probably by Bernardo Rossellino.

Bernardo Rossellino, view of second cloister

View of first cloister with the Pazzi Chapel

CIMABUE

Crucifix
circa 1288
Large refectory

The large *Crucifix* by Cimabue is considered one of the fundamental works of Italian art and a reference point for fourteenth-century painters, beginning with Cimabue's own pupil, Giotto. Although it was irreparably damaged by the 1966 flood, patient restoration of the pictorial fabric has allowed evidencing with great clarity how Cimabue had by this time broken definitively with the canons of Byzantine painting. The slack, seemingly inert body, the face with half-open eyes, the cut of the mouth, the vertical drop of the blood falling in clots, all show a sensitivity to natural fact that is exalted in rich chromatic tones and an impression of great composure. His architectural conception and non-random measures, heedful of precise proportional relationships, has been viewed as the link between this work and the Franciscan church of Santa Croce. Even though the painting has been documented with certainty as far back as 1288, and the church was begun only in 1294, Cimabue, who had already worked for this order at Assisi, must have already had the church design quite clear in his mind whilst executing the painting.

DONATELLO

Saint Louis of Toulouse
1423
Large refectory

The statue in gilded bronze was part of the tabernacle of the Guelph faction on the eastern side of the church of Orsanmichele. The shrine was later acquired and filled with the sculptural group of *Christ and Saint Thomas* by Verrocchio (p. 144). Shaped, cast and gilded in different pieces, as dictated by its dimensions, *Louis of Toulouse*, patron saint of the Guelph faction, turns slowly and solemnly, pivoting on the pastoral staff and giving evidence to the unfurling of his Episcopal robes. In the act of blessing, the young face, directed imperceptibly upward, shows the thrill of ecstatic rapture, and the gleaming of the gold that makes the figure stand out from the shadow of the niche is transformed into the light of sanctity.

TADDEO GADDI

Last Supper, Crucifixion, Stigmata of Saint Francis, Saint Louis of Toulouse serving table to the poor, Angel ordering the priest to bring food to Saint Benedict in the desert, Supper in the Pharisee's house

circa 1345-1350
Large refectory

This grandiose fresco occupying the back wall of the refectory was so damaged by the 1966 flood that its detachment from the underlying support was inevitable. The single scenes unfold within an illusory architectural-decorative structure bearing the Manfredi family coats of arms, surrounding the complex central *Crucifixion*. Inspired by the essay, *Lignum Vitae* by San Bonaventura da Bagnoregio, the *Tree of Life* is a pivotal theme in Franciscan meditation, which reached its maximum expression in the painting on wood panel by Pacino di Buonaguida, now in the Accademia Gallery (p. 41). In this fresco, Saint Francis, accompanied on the left by Saint John and the traditional group of Pious Women, as well as by other Franciscan saints on the right, embraces the cross, from which stem twelve branches terminating in racemes portraying the prophets and four evangelists. The allegorical meaning is explained in the scroll ornaments. The fact that the woman kneeling behind Saint Francis has been identified with some certainty as Monna Vaggia Manfredi, who commissioned the work and died in 1345, together with stylistic considerations, helps establish the dating of the fresco. Therefore, it was most likely executed in the mature years of Taddeo Gaddi, the official heir of Giotto in Florence, who brought this vast decoration to conclusion with the help of his thriving workshop and a learned Franciscan for the iconography.

Pazzi Chapel

The Pazzi Chapel, admirably enclosed within the cloister of Santa Croce, is one of the most celebrated buildings of the Renaissance. Designed and begun by Filippo Brunelleschi, its construction was carried on by collaborators after his death in 1446. It was still unfinished after the Pazzi family was banished from Florence for having conspired against the Medici in 1478. A capitular classroom equipped with a long bench running along its perimeter, the chapel, though limited in its extension by the pre-existing buildings, is a miracle of proportions whose exterior strikes a harmonious balance with the massive imposing structure of the Basilica. Thus, it represents the perfect, conclusive resolution of space according to the canons of Brunelleschi's genius. Embellishing the architecture's exterior are the at-

tic frieze with cherub heads, attributed to Desiderio da Settignano, the elaborate decoration of the small dome of the portico and the relief with Saint Andrew above the door by Luca della Robbia, who was perhaps aided by his nephew, Andrea, in carrying out the interior roundels of the Apostles, and finally, the roundels in the dome's pendentive, executed in rigorous adherence to perspective principles, so as to constitute a fitting completion to the architecture – a reply, perhaps, from the selfsame Brunelleschi to Donatello who had invaded his votive chapel in San Lorenzo with plaster-work (p. 148). It is precisely within the sober interior that once can appreciate how the space is both rigorously and geometrically proportionate, and how even the very light coming from the oculi in the cupola's drum and the portico falls as if to exalt the quality of the structure.

MUSEO DELL'OPIFICIO DELLE PIETRE DURE

Table top with vase of flowers, 1874

In 1588 grand duke Ferdinando I founded the Opificio, or Gem Workshop, which at the time was called "the Works Gallery" specialising in *commessi*, as were called the mosaic compositions of precious and semi-precious stones cut in sections of varying shapes which were then fitted so closely that the joints were barely invisible. True 'sto-

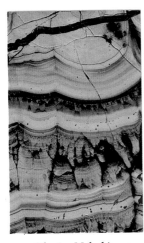

Siberian Malachite   **Persian lapis lazuli**   **Persian lapis lazuli**   **Persian lapis lazuli**

Melchizedek at the Arc, early 17th C

ne paintings', such works exploited the exquisite natural chromatic range of the rare and precious gems chosen for their making. The Opificio was originally located in the Uffizi before being transferred in the late 18th Century by grand duke Pietro Leopoldo of Lorraine to its current location in the former convent of San Niccolò di Cafaggio. Many fine works were produced here, amongst which: wall panels such as those in the Chapel of Princes (p. 65), intarsia panels for tables, chessboards, cabinets and other furnishings, greatly appreciated throughout Europe for their high quality and pleasant motifs , flowers and countrysides, as well as sacred scenes. With the birth of the new Italian State, the workshop continued its activities, though now self-financed through the sale of its creations to the public. At the turn of the century, decreasing demand for such objects prompted it to turn above all to the restoration of artwork. It was at this time that the museum was born, exhibiting the *commessi*, together with the tools and precious stones collected by the grand dukes, as testament to the history of this venerable age-old technique.

Sicilian jasper

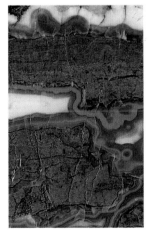

Spanish coral

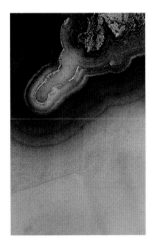

Agate sardonyx

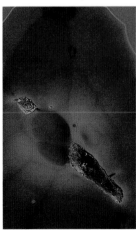

Goa Agate

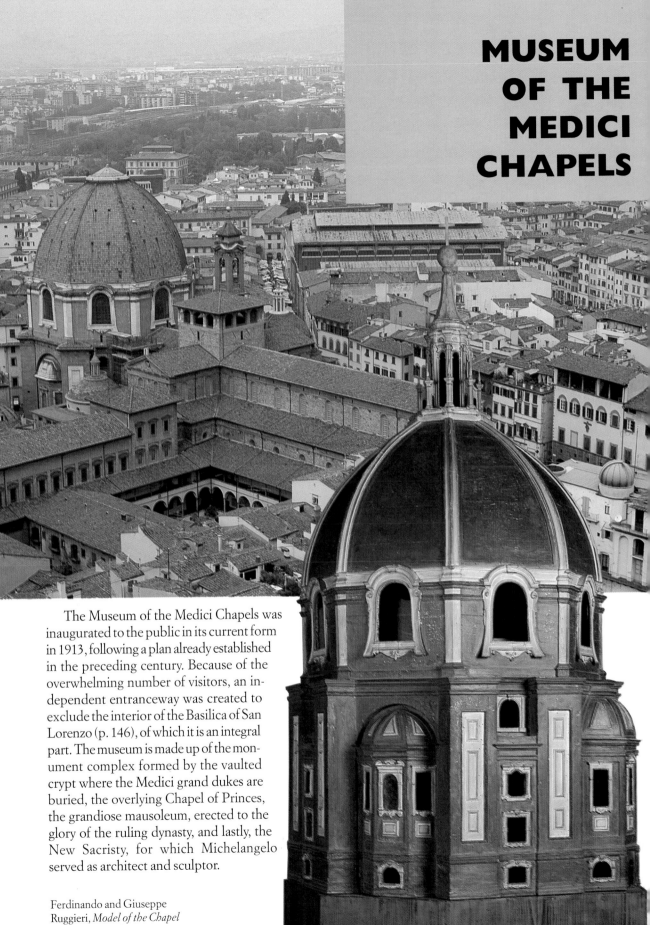

The Museum of the Medici Chapels was inaugurated to the public in its current form in 1913, following a plan already established in the preceding century. Because of the overwhelming number of visitors, an independent entranceway was created to exclude the interior of the Basilica of San Lorenzo (p. 146), of which it is an integral part. The museum is made up of the monument complex formed by the vaulted crypt where the Medici grand dukes are buried, the overlying Chapel of Princes, the grandiose mausoleum, erected to the glory of the ruling dynasty, and lastly, the New Sacristy, for which Michelangelo served as architect and sculptor.

Ferdinando and Giuseppe Ruggieri, *Model of the Chapel of Princes,* wood, ca. 1740

Chapel of Princes

Crossing the crypt – beneath which lie the underground passages of San Lorenzo, created by Brunelleschi and harbouring the tombs of Cosimo il Vecchio and Donatello – two flights of stairs lead to the Chapel of Princes. Already conceptualised by Cosimo I, its realisation was later promoted by his son Ferdinando I, who in 1602 called for a competition to determine who would secure the prestigious commission. The architect Matteo Nigetti resulted victorious, and espousing the design of Don Giovanni de' Medici, oversaw its construction until 1649. The work progressed slowly: the facing of the octagon with precious materials, destined to inspire awe in visitors then as now, drained the coffers of the Medici grand duchy. At the behest of the last descendant of the Medici house, Anna Maria Ludovica, the architects Ferdinando and Giuseppe Ruggieri finished the vault of the cupola, covered its exterior in *pietra forte* and white marble and added windows in the dome's drum, though the ribbing and lantern that were to make it resemble the cupola of Santa Maria del Fiore were never com-

Pietro Benvenuti,
Vault of the Chapel of Princes
illustrating Scenes from the
Old and New Testament

pleted. The intrados was frescoed between 1828 and 1837 with *Scenes from Genesis and the New Testament* by the neoclassical painter Pietro Benvenuti. The chapel, however, was completed only in the 20th Century: the altar, with semi-precious stone panels of varying provenance and periods, was reassembled in 1937, and the floor brought to completion in 1962 by the Opificio delle Pietre Dure (p. 62-63), which was founded by the grand duke Ferdinando in 1588 and has been engaged in decorating the chapel for over three centuries. In celebration of the power and majesty of the Medici dynasty, rich marble and semi-precious stone were used for the wall facings and frieze decorations, the latter bearing the coats of arms of the sixteen major cities of Tuscany, a sign of homage to the supremacy of the grand duchy. The names of all the grand dukes, from Cosimo I to Cosimo III, excepting therefore the last, Gian Gastone, are set in intarsia above the six niches, each of which holds a cenotaph. Only two of the six gilded bronze statues called for by the original design were ever carried out, those of Ferdinando I and Cosimo II, both depicted by Pietro and Ferdinando Tacca in the robes of Grand Masters of the Order of Saint Stephen.

Pietro and Ferdinando Tacca,
Ferdinando I, 17th C

New Sacristy

In 1520, after rescinding the contract for the façade of San Lorenzo, Pope Leo X and his cousin Giulio de' Medici entrusted Michelangelo with the execution of a funeral chapel near the church's northern transept. The chapel was destined to host an altar and the tombs of Lorenzo il Magnifico, his brother Giuliano, Lorenzo, the duke of Urbino, and Giuliano, duke of Nemours. The election of Cardinal Giulio to the papacy, under the name of Pope Clement VII in 1523, provided impetus to the work on the New Sacristy, subsequently interrupted a number of times following the dramatic events that were eventually to lead to the Sack in Rome in 1527, the establishment of the Republic of Florence and, eventually, the definitive re-entry of the Medici. When in 1534 Pope Clement VII died and Michelangelo moved to Rome, the Sacristy was still not complete, though the architecture and the statues were. It was therefore Vasari and Ammannati, by will of Cosimo I, who finished the work. The cubic space surmounted by a semicircular lacunar dome, which though symmetrical to the Old Sacristy by Brunelleschi (p. 148), to which it aspires, reveals an innovative design in which the *pietra serena* structures exhibit a plasticity and highly dramatic tension quite unlike the serene fifteenth-century equilibrium. On the wall devoid of marble facing is found the *Madonna and Child*, set on a simple base. Here the corpses of Lorenzo il Magnifico and his brother, Giuliano, were laid to rest in 1559, Michelangelo never having completed their funeral monuments. On either side of the Madonna are set the statues of the patron saints of the Medici, Saint Cosmas to the left and Saint Damian to the right, the respective work of Giovan Angelo da Montorsoli and Raffaello da Montelupo, two of Michelangelo's collaborators. The two dukes – both men of arms who died untimely – are accompanied by allegories of all-consuming Time. Their gaze is turned toward the Madonna, who is portrayed in a 'serpentine' pose, embracing the Child who bears the hope of Man's salvation.

Wall of the New Sacristy with *Madonna and Child with saints Cosmas and Damian*

To the right is Giuliano, Lorenzo il Magnifico's third-born and Pope Leo x's brother, portrayed as *condottiere* decisively turning his head: according to the neo-Platonic doctrines adhered to by Michelangelo, he represents Action – the active life incarnate. On the left he is flanked by smooth-bodied *Night*, illuminated as if by moonlight, while on the right stands *Day*, who face is unfinished.

Michelangelo Buonarroti,
*Tomb of Giuliano de' Medici,
duke of Nemours*

Above:
Michelangelo Buonarroti,
Night, detail

At left:
Michelangelo Buonarroti,
Day, detail

Michelangelo Buonarroti,
Dawn, detail

Michelangelo Buonarroti,
Dusk, detail

Michelangelo Buonarroti, *Tomb of Lorenzo de' Medici, duke of Urbino*

On the opposite wall is the duke of Urbino, Lorenzo, nephew of Lorenzo il Magnifico, portrayed in a meditative pose representing the contemplative life, Thought; at his feet, on the left, is *Dusk*, about to drowse off, and on the right, reawakening *Dawn*.

At left:
Roman manufacture, *Pastoral staff,* early 16th C, silver

Below:
Florentine manufacture, *Mitre,* early 16th C, pearl and gem-studded embroidery

Below:
Massimiliano Soldani Benzi, *Reliquary of Saint Casimir,* 1687, silver

The Treasure of San Lorenzo

As the Medici were the patrons of the Basilica of San Lorenzo, over the centuries it benefited from many donations: reliquaries and others liturgical articles from the most prestigious workshops in Florence, as well as the masterpieces of the Opificio delle Pietre Dure (p. 62-63). This Treasure was originally kept in the tribune on the church's inner façade, built after Michelangelo's design, where they were put on display for veneration by the faithful during particularly important ceremonies. Part of this Treasure is now displayed in the showcases located in the crypt and two rooms behind the altar of the Chapel of Princes (p. 65). There are rock crystal vases once belonging to Lorenzo il Magnifico and donated to the church by his second-born Pope Leo X, who hoped to establish his father's myth and consolidate the family prerogative over the basilica. In fact, it was he who also commissioned and donated the pearl and gem-studded *Mitre* and the exquisite, gilded silver *Pastoral staff* with Saint Lawrence within the loop of the laurel branch. Giovan Battista Foggini and Massimiliano Soldani Benzi, Cosimo Merlini and Giuseppe Antonio Torricelli were instead the authors of the baroque masterpieces.

MUSEUM OF CASA BUONARROTI

MICHELANGELO BUONARROTI
Battle of the Centaurs
1490-1492
First floor, Room 11

This marble relief was begun by Michelangelo in 1490, on commission to Lorenzo il Magnifico and was interrupted in 1492, probably due to the death of the latter, though the sculptor likely continued working on it for more than a decade after 1494. It is, in fact, incomplete, as evidenced by its unsculpted upper portion and the chisel marks visible on all the figures. The subject was suggested by Agnolo Poliziano, even though it was a theme dear to the Florentine cultural ambience of the late 15th Century. Michelangelo chooses a style calculated more to communicate strength and movement, than to narrate the mythological episode, in which the drunken and lascivious Centaurs interrupt the Lapiti wedding reception. The artist, though young in age, exhibits such technical mastery that Vasari extolled the work, saying it seemed "not by the hand of youth" but, on the contrary, revealed the hand "of a consummate Master". According to his biographers, Michelangelo himself always remained very attached to the sculpture.

In 1508, Michelangelo acquired some property in via Ghibellina where he lived from 1516 to 1525. Even after moving, first to the San Lorenzo quarter, then to Rome, he always entertained the idea of bequeathing to Florence a building linked to his name. His goal was never realised during his lifetime, given that his only descendant, his nephew, Leonardo, carried out only a limited restructuring of the property and had the current building constructed only in 1590. It was Leonardo's son, Michelangelo Buonarroti il Giovane (the young), an eminent figure in the cultural life of the city, who gave the building its current appearance and furthermore, in celebration of his illustrious ancestor, had the four monumental rooms created on the piano nobile (first floor), where a significant collection of 17th-century Tuscan art is exhibited. After various vicissitudes, the building was finally left to the city by the last of the Buonarotti house, Cosimo, who died in 1858. In 1859 the building was inaugurated to the public as a museum for the art and archaeology collection of the Buonarroti family. It holds, not only important works of sculpture and numerous sketches by Michelangelo, but also an interesting collection of Etruscan and Roman antiquities. Moreover, the rooms of the building preserve paintings after the taste of Michelangelo il Giovane, as well as majolicas, Robbiaware and coin collections.

MICHELANGELO
BUONARROTI

Madonna of the Steps
circa 1490
First floor, Room 11

This relief was executed in about 1490, when Michelangelo was only fifteen and studying in the home of Lorenzo il Magnifico. The execution in the "stiacciato" style makes clear his reference to the work of Donatello, the fifteenth-century sculptor who developed this technique in order to be able to render graded background planes within the limited thickness of the bas-relief, yielding an effect of greater depth. Michelangelo adopts the technique out of his spiritual affinity to, and admiration for his illustrious predecessor. However, as Vasari has already noted, Michelangelo's figures go further: they reveal "more grace and more design" as well as innovations not at all in conformity with the traditional rules of perspective, such as the flattening of the perspective to impart great visibility to the figures in the second plane. The work owes its name to the staircase on which two children seem to dance, while a third hangs a long cloth, helped by the third, just visible to the extreme right behind the dominant figure of the Madonna.

GALLERY
Room 18

Between 1613 and 1635 Michelangelo Buonarroti il Giovane, Michelangelo's nephew's son, had this gallery built and decorated to pay homage to his illustrious ancestor. It holds a famous collection of 17th-century Florentine painting. The room's floor is done in polychrome 'Montelupo' majolica panels and intarsia doors after a sketch by Pietro da Cortona. It contains works by all the most important artists of the time, from Empoli a Passignano and Bilivert to Matteo Rosselli. The paintings and chiaroscuro oils on the walls represent episodes in the life of Michelangelo, whilst the ceiling portrays scenes of the death and apotheosis of the artist, surrounded by allegories. Amongst these, the splendid canvas by Artemisia Gentileschi deserves special mention: the allegorical figure, the *Inclination*, is a nude female figure (later covered for the sake of 'decency') with compass in hand who gazes at the observer with a serene look and seductive carnality (panel 11). Completing the room's decorations are sculptures by Antonio Novelli (the effigy of Michelangelo) and Domenico Pieratti (Active and Contemplative Life personfied).

MUSEUM OF SAN MARCO

The Museum of San Marco is situated in the oldest part of the convent that was home to such illustrious Dominican friars as the sainted archbishop of Florence, Antonino Pierozzi (Saint Antoninus), the fierce preacher, Fra Girolamo Savonarola, as well as Beato Angelico and Fra Bartolomeo. It is a place that preserves Dominican traditions within a monumental, yet harmoniously proportioned space, rendered all the more meaningful by the many masterpieces of painting that so well express the spiritual climate of those times. The church and convent of San Marco date back to the late 13th Century and originally housed monks of the order of San Sylvester. By order of the Medici, the buildings were extensively remodelled by Michelozzo between 1436 and 1446 to receive the reformed Dominican order from Fiesole. Michelozzo, an architect in great favour with Cosimo il Vecchio, created a functional and modern convent complex centred on the cloister of San Antoninus, so called because the lunettes were frescoed in the early 17th Century with illustrations of the life of the saint. The three dormitory wings, containing cells frescoed by Beato Angelico and assistants, were designed by Michelozzo over pre-existing structures: the Chapter House, the Refectory and Hospice, where a large collection of Beato Angelico's paintings on wood panel has been housed since 1921. Two of the cells served as meditative retreat for Cosimo il Vecchio, who was very attached to the convent, so much so, that he donated the jewelled codices now found on the first floor of the library – today a true temple of Renaissance knowledge.

LORENZO MONACO
*"Noli me tangere",
Resurrection, Marys at the
Sepulchre*

BEATO ANGELICO
Deposition
1425-1432

Hospice

It was Palla Strozzi, the Florentine banker and rival of the Medici, who commissioned the panel from Lorenzo Monaco for his father's funeral chapel in the sacristy of Santa Trinita. In 1425 the painter died after having completed only the predella with *Stories of Saints Onofrio and Nicholas*, now in the Gallery of the Accademia, and the cusps with *"Noli me tangere"*, the *Resurrection* and *Marys at the Sepulchre*. The completion of the work was then entrusted to Fra Angelico, who painted the false pillars and *Deposition*, a subject well suited to the chapel's commemorative function. Rendered as a single unit, the landscape, suffused by a luminous atmosphere, goes beyond the traditional three-way partition of the scene so typical of medieval polytypchs. Solemn and tranquil in the eloquent gestures of the sacred representation, the characters don renaissance, and therefore modern clothing, in order to be identified by their characteristic, strong features. Thus, the man in the black headdress is thought to depict the architect and sculptor Michelozzo, the one holding the nails and crown of thorns is Palla Strozzi, who commissioned the work, and his son, Lorenzo, is the youth kneeing at his feet.

BEATO ANGELICO
Madonna enthroned with angels and saints ("Pala of San Marco")
1438-1443
Hospice

The altarpiece was painted by Beato Angelico for the high altar of the church of San Marco, remodelled by Michelozzo by will of Cosimo. The work is lacking its original frame and predella (divided up amongst various museums, only two panels remain here) and is unfortunately in a poor state of conservation (due to an early erosive cleansing that damaged the picture's surface). Nonetheless, it reveals the magnificence of Fra Angelico's rendition. The square panel, typical of Florentine renaissance altar pieces, reveals a heavenly gathering of the Enthroned Virgin and Child with angels and Saints Dominic, John the Evangelist, Mark, Francis, Damian and Peter, who are joined by Saints Cosmas and Lawrence, the patron saints of the Medici, kneeing in the foreground. The perspective depth is enhanced by the Anatolian carpet, perhaps inspired by those donated as gifts to the council that moved to Florence to 1439. The *Crucifixion*, which satisfied the traditional need to place a cross on the altar, is a picture within a picture.

BEATO ANGELICO
Lamentation
1436-1441
Hospice

The panel was begun by Beato Angelico in 1436 on commission to the Benedictine monk, Sebastiano Benintendi, and finished in 1441, as can be seen from the inscription on the Virgin's mantle. It was destined for the Compagnia della Croce al Tempio, a company devoted to comforting those condemned to death in their last hours before execution. Hence the choice of the theme of the *Lamentation*, which in addition to prompting meditation on Christ's sacrifice, represents an all too obvious allusion to the fate awaiting the convict. Outside the city wall, illuminated by an intense light and profiled by the regular sequence of its towers, looms the cross, at whose feet a group mourns the death of Christ. At the extreme right of the group, in mourning clothes, is beatified Villana delle Botti, Benintendi's ancestor.

BEATO ANGELICO
Linaioli Tabernacle
1433
Hospice

The *Tabernacle* was placed in the headquarters of the Linen-drapers' Guild who turned to Lorenzo Ghiberti for the marble frame, and Fra Angelico, who did the panel. The saints on the door panels, *Mark* and *Peter* on the outside, *John the Baptist* and once again *Saint Mark* on the inside, wear robes in the same flowing pattern as Ghiberti's sculptures. The Guild must have found pleasure in the richness of the clothing and the gold drapery that opens before the Madonna, executed on classic models of the *Maestà* of earlier centuries, though modernised through its plasticity and perspective clarity. In the predella, the *Sermon of Saint Peter in the presence of Saint Mark*, the *Adoration of the Magi* and the *Martyrdom of Saint Mark* are depicted in the background formed by city buildings, exhibiting a narrative vividness in the late gothic style.

79

Fra Bartolomeo

Madonna and Child with Saint Anne and other saints ("Pala of the Signoria")
1510-1513
Room of Fra Bartolomeo

This monumental altarpiece was commissioned in 1510 from the painter monk by the Gonfalonier of the Republic, Pier Soderini, who intended to place it on the altar in the room of the High Council in Palazzo della Signoria (p. 126) (hence the name). It was to celebrate the re-conquest of republican liberty after the Medici were ousted from the city government. The work, however, was still incomplete following the fall of the republic and consequent reinstatement of Medici rule in 1512 and the death of the painter in 1517. Although still in the preparatory stages, before the addition of colour, the altarpiece preserves all the majesty of the pyramidal composition that Fra Bartolomeo rendered after the design set forth by da Vinci, thus allowing full appreciation of the elegance of the lines and brightness of the lighting effects heightened by the chiaroscuro. The patron saints of Florence are depicted deliberating on the mystery of the Immaculate Conception with saints from the times when the city had achieved significant victories. Thus, according to Soderini's intent, the sacred conversation, set in a place such as the High Council, the forum for heated discussions, was to symbolise the return of democratic freedom.

Fra Bartolomeo

Portrait of Girolamo Savonarola
circa 1498-1499
Room of Fra Bartolomeo

Through the resolute look of the monk and the total lack of any background scene, the artist wishes to infuse the portrait with the character and ideals which, together with his fervent spirituality, were to drive Savonarola to follow his vocation and enter the Dominican order. The painter was in fact an impassioned follower of Savonarola, who lived at the convent of San Marco from 1484 up to his arrest in 1498 for heresy. Shortly thereafter, Savonarola was condemned to the stake as a heretic for his thundering sermons against Church corruption, lust and simony. An embarrassment to the Church because of the devotion he aroused in the populace, the monk foretold in fiery sermons of every kind of calamity for the city, were it not to amend its ways. The three areas of the convent that originally held Savonarola's chapel, study and cell contain relics and mementoes of his life.

BEATO ANGELICO
Crucifixion and Saints
1442
Chapter House

The Chapter House – where the monks gathered to debate decisions regarding the community and judge violations of the Rule – maintains its original fourteenth-century structure. Beato Angelico frescoed the back wall with the *Crucifixion and Saints*, which was intended more to prompt meditation on the Mystery of the Cross, rather than document the historical event. Serving as frame, the prophets of the Old Testament and a pagan sibyl lean out of the hexagonal windows with scroll ornaments to announce the advent and death of Christ. The painter does not indulge in any landscape detail whatever, so the group of saints stands out in full evidence against the sky, where the azurite paint has peeled off, allowing a glimpse at the underlying preparatory layer. Apart from the mourners, the saints linked to Florence and the Medici are depicted on the left – John the Baptist, Mark, Lawrence, Cosmas and Damian – while on the right are Saint Dominic, at the foot of the Crucifix, the Fathers of the Church, the founders of the main religious orders and finally two other Dominican saints, Peter Martyr and Thomas Aquinas. At the bottom, a winding vine shoot is upheld in the centre by Saint Dominic, the founder of the order whose history is represented by the portraits of its saints and canonised members in the circles on either side.

BEATO ANGELICO

Annunciation

circa 1440
Corridor of the clergy

The *Annunciation* is one of the few frescoes that Beato Angelico painted outside the monastic cells, the others being *Saint Dominic adoring the Crucifix*, on the opposite wall, and the *Sacred Conversation*, called the *Madonna of Shadows*, along the corridor onto which the rooms of the lay brothers open (the first one built by Michelozzo). The *Annunciation* was placed here to provide passing monks with the chance to meditate upon the mystery of the incarnation and, in keeping with the painting's black inscription, offer a prayer to the Virgin. A spiritual

and intimate dimension animates the scene, set under a loggia suffused with light, simply plastered and profiled by columns with partly ionic and partly corinthian capitals, inspired by the contemporary architecture that Michelozzo was then applying to San Marco. On the right, the garden closed in by a fence leads beyond to a wood typical of the Tuscan hills. Paintings of this subject usually included the scene of Adam and Eve being cast from the Garden of Eden. Here, however it is lacking, as everything is centred on the announcement that the angel is making to devout Mary seated on a rustic stool.

BEATO ANGELICO

The mocking of Christ with the Virgin and Saint Dominic
1438-1443
Corridor of the lay brothers, cell 7

Here, Beato Angelico offers for the contemplation of the erudite Dominican monk who occupied this cell a fresco depicting the *Mocking of Christ*, introducing into the foreground the sorrowful, self-absorbed Virgin Mother and young Saint Dominic, intent on his reading. In a courtyard awash with intense light, Christ, king of the Jews, sits on a throne covered in regal purple, while another green draping is hung behind him like a tapestry. His eyes are covered by a transparent blindfold, while the symbols of power, a reed and globe, are offered to him by his mockers, so unworthy as to be represented only by their gestures: hands appear that strike, slap and tip a hat in mock reverence, and a face spitting in his. And Christ acquiesces, invested with the candour of innocence, awaiting his imminent glory.

DOMENICO GHIRLANDAIO

Last Supper
1479-1480
Small refectory

In our path through the museum we have already encountered the large refectory, an area of monumental proportions and part of the convent's original medieval structure, though subjected to traumatic 16th-century work by which it was enlarged and decorated with the fresco of *Saint Dominic and his brothers fed by angels*, painted by Antonio Sogliani in 1536. The small refectory, on the other hand, was built ex novo by Michelozzo and, was eventually given over, to housing guests at the Dominican convent. The frescoing was entrusted to Domenico Ghirlandaio, who together with his brother, David, had already painted a refectory in the monastery at Badia a Passignano. Here, his work was evidently received with such satisfaction that he was called upon once again in 1480 to work on Ognissanti (p. 177). Above the corbel in the centre is a Crucifix, by now reduced to a barely visible vestige because it was painted onto already dry plaster. Through this detail the painter linked himself to the medieval tradition, which called for rendering the *Crucifixion* together with the *Last Supper*. The scene is depict-

ed under an open loggia, rich in symbolic elements alluding to the Passion and Resurrection of Christ, and done in a careful study of nature revealing the artist's knowledge of Flemish painting. The diffuse lighting reveals the influence of Beato Angelico, whose work Ghirlandaio had had the opportunity to examine. The apostles, in a mute dialogue of gestures and looks, are gathered in an atmosphere of serene suspension. Judas sits on the foreground side of the table; near him is a cat, the symbol of Evil and nemesis of the *Domini canes*.

MUSEUM OF SANTA MARIA NOVELLA

The cloisters known as the "Chiostro Verde" and "Chiostro dei Morti", together with the Refectory and other sections of the convent, go to make up the Museum of Santa Maria Novella. Several important series of frescoes from the 14th to the 16th Centuries adorn it walls, performed by such artists as Andrea di Bonaiuto, Paolo Uccello and Bronzino's pupil, Alessandro Allori, who painted the *Manna in the desert*, near a fourteenth-century *Madonna with Child and saints* on the back wall of the Refectory. The refectory also contains the *Reliquary busts of Saints Anastasia and Mary Magdalene* performed in the workshop of Matteo Civitali in Lucca at the end of the 15th Century. Older still are the two *Reliquary busts of Saint Ursula* from Senese school of the 14th Century. The *Relic of the title of the Cross*, is on display within a Venetian crystal shrine in the adjoining room, once the chapel of the Ubriachi family, which also holds the sinopie by Paolo Uccello and thirty-five 14th-century frescoes detached from the church's main chapel.

Paolo Uccello

*Stories of the Genesis
Stories of Noah*

circa 1431 and circa 1446
Chiostro verde

The frescoes, which have been transferred to canvas, were performed by Paolo Uccello in *terraverde* (a particular iron oxide and silicic acid based pigment, hence the name, "green cloister") on the second alcove on the eastern side (therefore the first the monks passed as they left church). They represent four scenes from Genesis: the *Creation of animals* and the *Creation of Adam*, and below, the *Creation of Eve* and *Original Sin*. The painter appears to have been influenced by Lorenzo Ghiberti, with whom he worked on the first door of the Florentine Baptistery, as well as by Masaccio, in the nude figure of Adam, and Masolino, in Eve's head as she confers with the serpent. Many of the naturalistic details, for instance, the sharp rocks and blooming garden, are clearly of the late gothic tradition. The later *Stories of Noah*, performed after the painter's stay in Padua, reveals a complex perspective layout that sacrifices the principles of realism, resulting in a more abstract effect. In the *Flood and Recession of the Waters*, Uccello imparts a rather daring foreshortening to the ark to produce a scene of great power, described by Vasari in these words: "the dead, the storm, the fury of the winds, the bolts of lightning, the uprooting of trees and the fear in the men". In the scene of the *Sacrifice*, the hovering God the Father, also foreshortened, almost seems to break down the wall before him.

*The flood and recession of the
waters, Sacrifice and
drunkenness of Noah*

ANDREA DI BONAIUTO

Triumph of Saint Thomas Aquinas, the Passion of Christ, Crucifixion and Descent into Limbo, Triumph of the Church, Stories of Saint Peter Martyr
1367-1369
Cappellone degli Spagnoli

On the northern side of the Chiostro Verde is the Chapter House of the Dominican convent, called the Cappellone degli Spagnoli (chapel of the Spaniards) because in 1540 it was granted by duke Cosimo I as a place of worship to the Spanish community who arrived with the entourage of Eleonora of Toledo. It was built in the late 14th Century by Jacopo Talenti, thanks to the magnanimity of Branda and Mico Guidalotti. Then, between 1367 and 1369, Andrea di Bonaiuto, fresco painter of good will and great pedagogic aptitude, painted a complex series of frescoes to the glorification of the Dominican order, defender of the Church and the Christian doctrine in the struggle against heresy. On the eastern wall, where the *Triumph of the Church* is depicted, one can see the Florentine cathedral after a design prepared in 1367 for a commission on which the painter also worked. On the opposite wall is the *Triumph of Saint Thomas Aquinas*, depicting the Church's most eminent scholar at the pulpit of wisdom, and the *Allegory of the Arts and Sciences* which figuratively translates the Thomistic concept of knowledge on which the Studio di Santa Maria Novella was founded. The northern wall is frescoed with Christ's *Passion*, *Crucifixion* and *Descent into Limbo*, which corresponds on the opposite wall to *Stories of Saint Peter Martyr*, damaged by modifications made in the late 16th Century.

Triumph of Saint Thomas Aquinas

DIOCESAN MUSEUM OF SANTO STEFANO AL PONTE

The annexes of Santo Stefano al Ponte were originally used to store works of art from churches in the city and surrounding areas that were no longer administered by the Florentine archdiocese. In 1993, following the car bombing of May 27, the works contained in the Museo del Seminario Maggiore were brought here, and the damaged works restored and displayed, thus transforming it from temporary storehouse to museum in its own right. In the oratory of the Company of the Holy Sacrament the rite of the Mass is reconstructed, performed by wooden manikins wearing ancient vestments. In the adjoining Chapel of the Goldsmiths, 15th-century paintings are displayed near gold-back paintings from the late 14th to early 15th Century, and the receptacles along the corridor hold precious works of jewellery. The sacristy, which still preserves its sixteenth-century benches, contains the museum's most important work, the *Virgin enthroned* by Giotto, from the church of San Giorgio alla Costa and dated to between 1295 and 1300. Also found here is the predella, with the *Adoration of the Magi*, attributed to Paolo Uccello, and the panel with Masolino's *Saint Julian*, part of a triptych that the painter executed in collaboration with Masaccio for Santa Maria Maggiore. Part of this predella is now in the Horne Museum (p. 88).

Giotto, *Virgin enthroned*

In his last will and testament, Herbert Percy Horne (1864-1916), English architect and art collector, left the building in via de' Benci and the collection it contained to the Italian State. He had acquired the building in 1911 and had it restored with the intention of recreating the ambience of a Renaissance home. The building originally belonged to the Alberti family, who had it built in the mid 14th Century. In 1489 it passed over into the hands of the Corsi family, who restructured it in Renaissance style – the work being done by Simone del Pollaiolo, know as Cronaca, or perhaps his student, Baccio d'Agnolo. The rustication of the entrance, windows and corners climbs upward in strong relief from the austere plaster façades. Within the ground-floor courtyard, on the northern side, is a portico with elegant capitals, created by Andrea Sansovino, and a two-storey loggia. The museum boasts an important collection of coins, ceramics and sculpted furniture, a curious and rare collection of tableware from the 13th to 18th Centuries, and sculptures in wood, marble, plaster and terracotta. Lastly, the painting collection includes Giotto's *Saint Stephen*, Pietro Lorenzetti's triptych, a predella compartment with *Stories of Saint Julian* by Masaccio, as well as a tondo by Domenico Beccafumi, with a monumental frame and, not least, the works of Dosso Dossi and Francesco Furini.

GIOTTO
Saint Stephen
circa 1320
First floor, room II

By now, art historians generally agree on attributing this work to Giotto. It is part of a polyptych, probably originally from one of the transept chapels of Santa Croce. In fact, its plasticity and colouring are typical of the painter's work during in the third decade of the 14th Century, when he was engaged in decorating Santa Croce, first in the Peruzzi Chapel (p. 156) and then on the frescoes of the Bardi Chapel (p. 157). Here, Saint Stephen wears a deacon's habit; on his head are two stones, attributes of the saint who was stoned after incurring the wrath of the Hebrews assembled in the Sanhedrim by accusing them of killing the Messiah.

ANTONIO ROSSELLINO
Madonna of the candelabra
circa 1470
Second floor, room IV

The sculpture in polychrome plaster work is thought to be the work of Antonio Rossellino, who also executed the marble masterpiece that can be admired in the chapel of the Cardinal of Portugal in the church of San Miniato al Monte (p. 152). The sculptor was helped in carrying out the relief by Neri di Bicci, a Florentine painter who managed a prosperous workshop. Numerous copies are know to exist, testimony to the fact that such images of personal religious worship were very much in demand. They could in fact be easily produced at modest cost by casting from models, and then painted or embellished according to the price the buyer was willing to pay.

BARGELLO NATIONAL MUSEUM

The Bargello National Museum has its centre in the building that was erected in the mid 13th Century as the headquarters for the powerful political offices of the Capitano del Popolo, and later, in 1261, the Podestà. The stark construction was enlarged during the 14th Century from its original core on via del Proconsolo toward via dell'Acqua, with the consequent addition of an austere courtyard embellished by gothic elements, such as the single and double lancet windows and merlons. Between 1345 and 1367, the courtyard staircase leading to the upper floor was constructed, from which the beautiful loggia, dubbed *Verone*, can be admired. The building has always been linked to Florentine civil life and the administration of justice, so much so, that in the 15th Century the Medici used to have the effigies of their political adversaries painted on the walls, side by side with those of common criminals. Between 1502 and 1574, the building housed the Giudici della Ruota, while the advent of the Capitano di Piazza, named "Bargello", led to the darkest period of the building's history. It was, in fact, transformed into a prison, and its large rooms, courtyard and even the Cappella della Maddalena, which Vasari attributes to Giotto, given over to cells or the service of its new penal function. Only in the mid-19th Century, when the prison was transferred elsewhere, did the slow but progressive recovery of the building begin, the results of which we can admire today. The fame of the portrait of Dante in the frescoes of the Cappella della Maddalena contributed to the building's reclamation, and during the 1865 celebrations in honour of the poet, the National Museum was founded. It grew progressively thanks in part to the suppression of ecclesiastical institutes and, above all, to the donations of collectors and patrons (such as Louis Carrand in 1888, Costantino Ressman in 1899 and Giulio Franchetti in 1907). It now boasts a magnificent collection of Florentine sculpture and applied arts set in a medieval atmosphere where the echoes of the ancient violence and torture have finally been silenced.

MICHELANGELO BUONARROTI
Drunken Bacchus
1496-1497
Michelangelo Room

An early work, Bacchus was commissioned from Michelangelo in 1496, during his first stay in Rome, by cardinal Raffaello Sansoni Riario. The statue was to be placed in a courtyard at the cardinal's residence at the Chancellery Building, together with other classical sculptures. However, the cardinal, perhaps perplexed by the unusual, sensual representation of the divinity, disliked it. Caught in a moment of seeming imbalance, *Bacchus*, by now overcome by the nectar's intoxicating effects, lifts a wine cup with a complacent, lascivious expression, while behind him a mischievous little satyr tries to eat the grapes in his left hand. The body, modelled with the agile musculature of a young man, nevertheless has a sensual, almost feminine fleshiness about it. Sold by the cardinal to the banker Iacopo Galli, the statue was later acquired by the Medici in 1570, probably prompted by the opinion of Vasari, who judged it to be an admirable work, referring to it as a "momentous mixing of marvellous members".

**MICHELANGELO
BUONARROTI**

*Madonna and Child with
young Saint John
("Tondo Pitti")*
1504-1505
Michelangelo Room

This masterpiece was made by the still young Michelangelo between 1504 and 1505, once commission from Bartolomeo Pitti, member of the powerful banker family that had begun construction of the building which would later be acquired by the Medici (p. 100). According to Renaissance tradition, the tondo, whether, sculpted, as this one, or painted, as the one Michelangelo did for the Doni family (p. 26), served as a devotional article for the home. The three vigorous, yet delicate figures in the harmonious circular composition seem constrained within the small space, a fact that confers a monumental importance upon them. The different levels of relief, from the evident protrusion of the Madonna, to Saint John, who barely rises up from the background, together with the subjects' varying degrees of finish, create an almost chiaroscuro pictorial effect.

MICHELANGELO BUONARROTI

Brutus
1539-1540
Michelangelo Room

The bust depicting *Brutus*, the only example of its kind in Michelangelo's repertoire, was commissioned from the artist by Cardinal Ridolfi, an exponent of the anti-Medici party, who wished to immortalise his cousin Lorenzino, who assassinated Alessandro de' Medici in 1536, in the likeness of his illustrious forerunner, Caesar's assassin. Carefully avoiding the work's political overtones, Vasari, in his *Vite*, attributes the inspiration for the work to a portrait of Brutus carved in an ancient cornel tree. Despite its political message and the fact of its having been commissioned by mortal enemies, it was acquired in 1590 by the grand duke Ferdinando I de' Medici, who appreciated its superb quality. The face's rough surface is a typical example of Michelangelo's much-studied technique of the "unfinished".

BENVENUTO CELLINI

Cosimo I
1545-1547
Michelangelo Room

Despite its colossal dimensions, far larger than life, the bust of Cosimo I wearing classical armour adorned with small, finely detailed grotesques, reveals the skill in the art of goldwork that made Benvenuto Cellini so much in demand with popes and sovereigns alike. The sculpture was completed in 1547 and cast in bronze early the following year. Hand-finished by chiselling, after the model of Roman sculptures, and adorned in gild and silver, traces of which remain in the eyes, the bronze did not pleased the grand duke, who had it placed at the main entrance to the fortress of Portoferraio on the faraway island of Elba.

GIAMBOLOGNA
*Owl, eagle, turkey, barn
owl, cock, falcon, peacock,
lapwing and eaglet*
1567
Verone

The numerous bronze animals displayed
in the *Verone* loggia are part of the series
commissioned from Giambologna in
1567 by Francesco I de' Medici for the
grotto of Villa di Castello. The various
birds are represented with naturalistic
precision in the rendering of their
plumage and postures that highlight their
characteristic features: the rather awkward
haughtiness of the turkey (which was moreover
little known at the time, having been imported from the
New World), or the fixity of the owl's gaze, the nimble carriage of the eagle, poised on a rock while seeking out its prey,
and the aristocrat elegance of the peacock. The artist could
certainly have drawn inspiration for those sculptures from
the Medici menagerie, where wild animals were kept for the
hunt and games.

DONATELLO
David [marble]
1408
Donatello Room

The marble statue of *David*, originally painted and gilded, was commissioned in 1408 for one of the apsidal buttresses of the cathedral of Santa Maria del Fiore, where however it was never placed. Done early in the career of the artist, it is his first attempt at a statue of large dimensions. The reference to Lorenzo Ghiberti is evident in the graceful aspect of the figure, whose curved pose recalls characters in the gothic style, while the careful anatomical study of the hands are a prelude to *Saint George* (p. 96). The expressive aristocrat pride which Donatello imparts to the sculpted figure of the hero resulted in the statue's being acquired and placed in Palazzo della Signoria (p. 126) in 1416 as a symbol and model of virtue.

DONATELLO
David [bronze]
1440-1450
Donatello Room

The bronze *David*, with a meditative look and sensual body, harmoniously fashioned after the models of ancient deities, is depicted setting his foot limply on the bodiless head of his enemy. Nothing about him recalls the heroic daring so dominant in other renditions of David, the very symbol of freedom. In fact, a number of other inconsistent iconographic features, such as the hat, have even raised doubts as to whether it represents the biblical hero at all. The statue was sculpted on commission to the Medici for the courtyard of the family palace, whence it was confiscated in 1494, when the Florentine Republic was established, and placed in Palazzo della Signoria (p. 126).

DONATELLO
Saint George and Saint George and the Dragon (bas-relief)
1415-1417
Donatello Room

The statue of *Saint George*, arising with proud and heroic resoluteness within the towering niche, was commissioned in 1415 from Donatello by the Arte dei Corazzai e Spadai (Armourer's Guild) for its own shrine outside the church of Orsanmichele, from which it was removed in 1892. In extolling its qualities, Vasari defined it as "vivissima" (very much alive), an adjective that sums up the essential aspect of the work, which although originating in careful study of classical sculpture, nonetheless reveals an expressive strength typical of the Renaissance. The certainties of the renaissance man, in fact, come alive in the stance and determined look of the saint, who once bore a gilded metal sword in his right hand. The relief portraying God the Father in the crowning, and more so, the scene in the plinth, moved here in 1984, are two of the finest examples of the "stiacciato" technique through which the sculptor, by the grading of the planes, heightened perspective and created an almost pictorial softness.

ANDREA DELLA ROBBIA
Madonna and Child ("Architects' Madonna")
1475
Room of Andrea della Robbia

This scalloped tabernacle is the first documented work by Luca della Robbia's nephew, Andrea, to whom the uncle taught the secret of glazed terracotta, a technique in which he was to became undisputed master of the family workshop by about 1470. Apart from coats of arms, tabernacles, vault and wall coverings, and naturally statues, Andrea executed above all bas-reliefs of the Madonna and Child for articles of private worship, to which he imparted a tender, homelike narrative style that made them so successful. This Madonna, duplicated a number of times with slight variations, was commissioned by the Arte dei Maestri di Pietra e Legname (Stone and Wood Workers Guild) who wanted their symbols on porphyry discs in the lower portion of the frame, which was decorated on the other sides by a frieze of roses emerging from bean-motif vases. To affirm the mystery of the incarnation, in the background sky strewn with clouds and animated by cherubs projecting from the intrados, the dove of the Holy Spirit is sent forth from the hands of God the Father to descend upon the *Madonna and Child*.

VERROCCHIO

Dame of the bouquet

1475-1480
Verrocchio Room

This splendid portrait of a lady, which critics have incon-
clusively identified as either Ginevra de' Benci – due to the
evident similarities to the portrait by da Vinci – or as Lu-
crezia Donati, the beloved of Lorenzo il Magnifico, can be
attributed to Verrocchio's mature years. Up to then, portraits, like those in this same room, were cut at shoulder
height, following the traditions of Roman bust portraits and
gothic reliquaries. Here instead, Verrocchio sculpts the bust
as far down as the waist, also including the hands, done with
enchanting levity. This novelty was immediately praised by
contemporaries. The composed and delicate figure, whose
profile is outlined under nearly diaphanously veiled clothing, affectionately holds a bouquet of flowers to her breast,
while the sweet, serene face is framed by curls. The masterpiece was originally in the Uffizi, where it was considered to
be the work of Donatello.

GIAN LORENZO BERNINI

Bust of Costanza Bonarelli

1636
Room of Baroque Sculpture
and Medals Collection

Splendid example of 17th-century sculpture, this bust was
done by the artist for entirely private reasons – it represents
Costanza Bonarelli, the sculptor's lover. Its great expressive
power resides in the resolute look in the woman's face and
the sensual roundness of the forms, exalted by the admirable
sculpting and realistic reproduction of the blouse in disar-
ray. The work by Bernini was formerly held in the Uffizi,
where it was displayed for the sake of comparison side by
side with Michelangelo's *Brutus* and other, classical busts.

STIBBERT MUSEUM

The villa which houses the Stibbert Museum, and where its founder created this eclectic collection, is the product of the restructuring of two pre-existing buildings, surrounded by a suggestive park in the romantic style. The English-born Frederick Stibbert (1838-1906) was an international financier, painter, impassioned student of art and popular customs and an eminent figure in the English community of late 19th-century Florence. This collection, fruit of Stibbert's singular passion, was reorganised in 1883, and now unfolds according to the various traditions, weapons and heraldic types throughout the rooms of the villa – restructured several times by Stibbert himself, notably in 1879 and 1905. An interesting testimony to nineteenth-century museum collection, it boasts many rare pieces, such as the table with malachite top in the Imperial style of Philippe

Room of the Cavalcade

Burial breastplate of Giovanni dalle Bande Nere, southern Germany, circa 1520
Room of the Cavalcade

Malachite-topped table, Malachite Room

Napoleon's Italian coronation uniform, Imperial Loggia

Thomire, as well as suggestive exhibits, like the famous *Cavalcade* in the armoury, where weapons, armours and horses harnessed according to the European tradition are displayed in theatrical pomp. There is also a rich collection of oriental weapons, jewels, renaissance furniture, western and oriental furnishings, tapestries, precious jewellery and an important collection of liturgical paraments. The Imperial Loggia contains, amongst other treasures, Napoleon Bonaparte's Italian coronation uniform . The paintings include, apart from several panels from the fourteenth-century school, works of important masters, such as the *Predella* fragment by Neri di Bicci and *Mary Magdalene* by Alessandro Allori.

Cavalryman's armour, mixed, Mameluke and Ottoman manufacture, Turkey, late 15th - early 16th C
Gilded steel with silver engravings and *repoussage* work
Room of the Cavalcade

PITTI PALACE

It was Luca Pitti, rival banker of the Medici, who began construction of the building on the hill of Boboli after a design, it is said, by Filippo Brunelleschi. At that time, toward the mid-15ᵗʰ Century, the building was a single block with a double tier of seven windows and three entranceways. A century later, it was acquired by Cosimo I de' Medici, at the insistence of his consort, Eleonora of Toledo. Bartolomeo Ammannati was entrusted with transforming the building into a suitable palace for the new court residence. From 1558 to 1570 he modified the façade by adding the Michelangelo-inspired "inginocchiate" windows at the two side entrances and built the courtyard with two wings and main balcony facing the garden (p. 122), which was also undergoing modifications. The court then was transferred from Palazzo Vecchio (p. 126), as it has come to be called ever since, to the new residence. Its expansion in the lengthwise direction continued during the 17ᵗʰ Century, first with Giulio Parigi and then his son Alfonso, so that the façade began to take on its current imposing dimensions. The two rondos, or side wings, were added subsequently, during the rule of the Lorraine who took over from the Medici in 1737 after the last Medici, Gian Gastone died without heirs. The new ruling dynasty had the Palazzina della Meridiana built upon an extension to the building's south wing, and continued the decoration of the rooms. This had begun toward the end of 16ᵗʰ Century in the rooms that make up the so-called apartment "of the Tapestries", but it was during the grand duchy of Ferdinando II that the summer quarters on the ground floor (now the Silverworks Museum) and

the winter apartments on the first floor (now the Palatine Gallery) were frescoed by Giovanni da San Giovanni and Pietro da Cortona in triumphal Baroque allegories replete with historical and mythological characters. When Florence became capital of the Kingdom of Italy (1865-1871), the court of Vittorio Emanuele II of Savoy had its centre in Pitti Palace. This was the third and last ruling house that the building would house, before it passed into the public domain in 1915 to become one of the most important museum complexes in Italy. It now houses the Silverworks Museum, Porcelain Museum, the Palatine Gallery and Royal Apartments, the Modern Art Gallery and Costume Gallery, as well as the Carriage Museum.

Silverworks Museum

The Silverworks Museum is located on the ground floor of Pitti Palace, in what was once the summer residence of the Medici grand dukes. All its rooms, with the exception of the entrance hall and Sala della Grotticina (small grotto) are fruit of the 17th-century expansion ordered by Cosimo II. The history of the museum began in the mid-19th Century, when the room frescoed by Giovanni da San Giovanni was used to store the treasures of the bishop-princes of Salzburg who arrived in Florence in 1814 with Ferdinando III of Lorraine. By century's end, porcelains were exhibited, then the jewels of Elettrice Palatina, just after her return from Vienna; then, in the 1920s, it was the furniture, precious stone vases, cameos and carvings from the Uffizi, and finally the ivories and ambers transferred here from the Bargello. Thus began the collec-

Below:
Public Hearing Room

At right:
Private Hearing Room

tion of myriad and varied precious, rare and sometimes bizarre objects, commissioned first by the Medici, then the Lorraine, or having other origins but transferred for dynastic reasons here, where the ruling dynasty lived a life of sophisticated luxury. And awe-inspiring indeed are not only the works collected here, but the setting itself, especially the exhibition rooms – whose windows open onto the façade – elaborately decorated with illusory effects: the antechamber of the Hearing Room, frescoed by Giovanni da San Giovanni and successors (1635-1642) as well as the successive three rooms by Angelo Michele Colonna and Agostino Mitelli (1637 and 1641).

GIOVANNI DA SAN GIOVANNI, CECCO BRAVO, FRANCESCO FURINI AND OTTAVIO VANNINI

All-consuming Time, Satyrs chasing Culture from Mount Parnassus, Meeting of the fugitives with Toscana, Lorenzo il Magnifico receives the Muses, Lorenzo talks to Prudence, Flora and Prudence, Lorenzo amongst the artists, Lorenzo and Faith, Lorenzo in the Careggi villa, Lorenzo's Death (walls)

Allegory of the wedding of Ferdinando II and Vittoria della Rovere, Flora admired by Pan, Love bringing the lion to pay respects to Mars (ceiling)
1635-1642
Room of Giovanni da San Giovanni

The room was the antechamber to the Sala d'Udienza (i.e., hearing room) where opulent banquets were held on special occasions. The frescoes were begun in 1635 by Giovanni da San Giovanni (hence its name) to celebrate the wedding of Ferdinando II with Vittoria della Rovere. The artist paints a self-portrait in the figure with the crab in hand, symbol of the astrological sign of Cancer. After the painter's death the decoration was continued and brought to completion in 1642 by San Giovanni's followers Francesco Furini, Ottavio Vannini and Cecco Bravo. The walls, which give the illusion of an airy loggia, bear episodes depicting the forerunner of the sixteenth-century grand dukes, Lorenzo il Magnifico, in his role of patron of the arts who made Florence the new Athens. On the ceiling, a wedding allegory is represented: the green twig of an oak, coat of arms of the Rovere family, is grafted onto the Medici blazon. Although his marriage to Vittoria della Rovere never earned Ferdinando the hoped for territorial expansion, her dowry contained great masterpieces which even today inspire the admiration of visitors to the Palatine Gallery and Uffizi.

FLORENTINE MANUFACTURE

Double cup

circa 1470
Sala Buia or
Hearing room of the grand duchess

Lorenzo il Magnifico's famous collection of precious stone vases (also including some having belonging to his father) was looted and scattered in 1494 when Lorenzo's son, Pietro, was exiled upon the arrival of the French troops of Charles VIII. The surviving pieces, often marked with the initials LAU.R.MED, (where the R is thought to stand for Rex), are divided amongst the Silverworks Museum, the Treasure of San Lorenzo and the Mineralogy Museum. This amethyst double cup has one end with a diamond-studded ring, the emblem of Lorenzo, and a ball emblazoned with round Medici bezants, one of which holds the French blazon (i.e., three golden lilies on blue background) which Piero il Gottoso received from Louis XI in 1465. The gilded silver edges are decorated entirely with small feathers similar to those on a hunting horn that once belonged to Lorenzo.

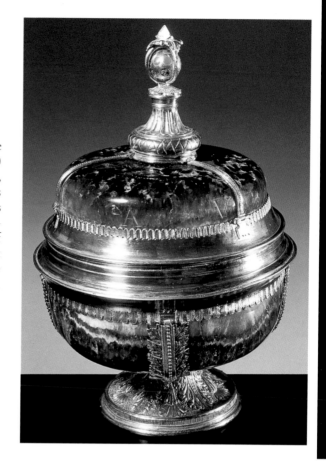

ULRICH BAUMGARTEN, JOHANN KÖNIG OR ANTON MOZART AND OTHERS

Cabinet called 'di Alemagna'

1619-1625
Public hearing room

Designed by Philipp Hainhofer, art merchant at Augsburg, this piece of furniture was acquired at an exorbitant price by the archduke of Tyrol, Leopoldo, who wished to give it to Ferdinando II de' Medici during the grand duke's journey to Innsbruck in 1628. Once placed in the Uffizi, the cabinet therefore came to be known as 'di Alemagna' (from Germany), a name evoking its origins that also served to distinguish it from other, similar ones made for Francesco I and Ferdinando I (today lost). The part sculpted in ebony is by Baumgarten, the precious stone panelling is miniated with biblical scenes and Episodes of the life of Christ. The drawers once contained stones and pearls. It has a revolving altar with amber figurines, *commessi* panels and, on the back, deforming mirrors. It is surmounted by a clock and contains a mechanical organ (today lacking its mechanism) that automatically played music composed by Christian Erbach. Certainly a mechanical wonder, its appearance as such is however secondary to its exuberant sacred iconography, in that it was meant to symbolise the Cosmos.

GRAND DUKE'S WORKSHOPS
(AFTER DESIGN BY GIOVAN BATTISTA FOGGINI)
Elector's cabinet
1709
Third State Room

Carved in ebony and precious stone in the workshops of the grand duke, it follows the design of Giovan Battista Foggini (Florence's most important baroque sculptor) and was commissioned by Cosimo III for his son-in-law, Johann Wilhelm von der Pfalz-Neuburg, the 'Palatine Elector', husband of Anna Maria Luisa de' Medici. The cabinet represents the apotheosis of Medici furniture, as Maria Luisa was to be the last descendant of the dynasty: in 1737 the grand duchy would pass to the Lorraine. In the centre of the niche is the gilded bronze statue of the Elector, surmounted by the combined coat of arms of the Medici and Pfalz. Originally, all the panels were embossed, but were replaced in the 19th Century with flat *commessi* mosaics.

VALERIO BELLI
Case
1532
Room of precious stones

In 1533 Pope Clement VII made a gift of this precious case to the king of France, François I, on the occasion of the wedding of his niece Caterina de' Medici, to the sovereign's second-born, who would succeed to the throne as Henry II. The enamelled ovals, in fact, bear the name and emblem of the Medici pope. Scenes of the Passion of Christ are sculpted in the rock crystal panels laminated at the back in silver, which acts as a support to enhance the incisions. The balanced architectural design and the unfolding of individual episodes reveal the full mastery of the stone engraver from Vicenza, Valerio Belli, whose name is engraved together with the date on the cover. A favourite of the Medici popes, Belli worked extensively in Rome during the papacies of both Leo X and Clement VII.

FLORENTINE MANUFACTURE AND JACQUES BILIVERT (DESIGNED BY BERNARDO BUONTALENTI)

Flask ("Buontalenti's Vase")
1583
Room of precious stones

One of the most meaningful works performed under Francesco I (as revealed by the initials F.M., the grand duke's coat of arms and the date beneath the base) it is the only one whose preparatory sketch remains. The design by Bernardo Buontalenti, the grand duke's favoured architect, was executed in the shops of Casino a San Marco, where the stone part in lapis lazuli was sculpted by Milanese artisans, while the fitting of the gold and enamel was performed by Jacques Bilivert, a Dutch goldsmith popular at the Medici court. This latter was also entrusted with carrying out the grand duke's crown. The elegant vase used to be held in the Uffizi together with other precious vases in materials such as jasper and rock crystal – the prides of the Medici collection for the technical excellence and supreme refinement so evident even today.

Pietro da Cortona, *Golden Age,* decoration of the Sala della Stufa, Palatine Gallery

Palatine Gallery and Royal Apartments

The grand staircase in the right corner of the courtyard of Pitti Palace leads to the Palatine Gallery, housed on the "noble" first floor of building's left wing, that which was once the Medici grand dukes' winter apartments, made up of the state rooms, the grand duke's living quarters in the back and those of the grand duchess in the wing called "Volterrano". In 1637 Ferdinando II called upon Pietro da Cortona, a painter in great favour in Rome, to fresco the walls of the Sala della Stufa (stove room) with the *Four ages of Man*. The work's joyful inventiveness and pleasant light colours prompted the grand duke to entrust him with decoration of the rooms on the façade. Dedicated to a divinity, they celebrate the Medici family in brilliant *trompe l'œil* perspective. The crowded figures at the edges thin out toward the centre to impart a sense of lightness that is further enhanced by the white and gilded plasters, integral part of the decoration supervised by the painter with the help of Ciro Ferri, who also completed the work when the maestro abandoned it, unfinished, in 1647. The rich decoration continues

Throne Room, Royal Apartments

in the furnishings and on the walls covered with paintings, arranged, not in chronological order or by school, but rather according to the symmetries of the splendid sculpted and gilded frames; therefore, according to exclusively decorative criteria. This is typical of baroque galleries, of which the Palatine is one of the world's greatest examples. Cosimo II began gathering the first core collection in 1620, which was enlarged by his son Ferdinando II, thanks above all to the dowry of his wife, Vittoria della Rovere. Subsequently, the collections of cardinal Leopoldo added paintings of the Venetian school, and those of prince Ferdinando, renaissance and baroque masterpieces. The Lorraine, who succeeded the Medici in 1737, also contributed much to the collection. In 1828 the first catalogue was drafted and the gallery opened to a select audience in the same rooms it is found today. The Room of Niches in the gallery leads to the first floor of the right wing, where the Royal Apartments are located. They became the official residence of Vittorio Emanuele II during the period when Florence was the capital of the Kingdom of Italy (1865-1871).

FILIPPO LIPPI

Madonna and Child with scenes from the life of Saint Anne ("Tondo Bartolini")

circa 1450
Prometheus Room

This splendid tondo was painted by Filippo Lippi in the mid 15th Century, not for the Bartolini family, as was once believed, but more likely for the Martelli family, whose coat of arms, a rampant griffon designed by the painter, can be seen on the back of the work. The Madonna is represented in the foreground with Child Jesus, who is offering her a pomegranate grain, a symbol of Christ's Passion. In the background, different moments in the life of Saint Anne are represented according to the medieval tradition, that is, all within the same undivided space: her meeting with Joachim (Mary's father) at the Golden Gate and the birth of the Virgin, amongst others. All unfolds in areas of vivid colours that, together with the rigorous use of perspective, serve to partition the space in which the wall, nearly a stage curtain, divides the bare outside scenes from the warmth of the house interior. The background scenes thus constitute a theological comment on the central theme of the Virgin and her purity, a much debated topic in those years.

RAPHAEL (RAFFAELLO SANZIO)

Madonna and Child, young Saint John and saints ("Madonna dell'impannata")

circa 1514
Ulysses Room

This work, painted for Bindo Altoviti, a wealthy Florentine banker at the Roman Curia, gets its name from the starched curtain (i.e., impannata) covering the window in the background to ward off the rigours of winter. Within simple domestic surroundings, the circular composition depicts the central figure of Child Jesus encircled by the group in the foreground. Evidently after much deliberation, Raphael decided to close the idealised circle by inserting the figure of Saint John on the right. This was at first testified to by a sketch in the Uffizi and recently confirmed by the x-ray studies performed for its restoration, which have in fact revealed that under the current figure of Saint John is a portrait of Saint Joseph holding a small John the Baptist in his arms. The panel bearing Raphael's autograph can be dated to about 1514, when the painter was engaged, together with others from his workshop, in frescoing the Stanza dell'Incendio di Borgo in the Vatican.

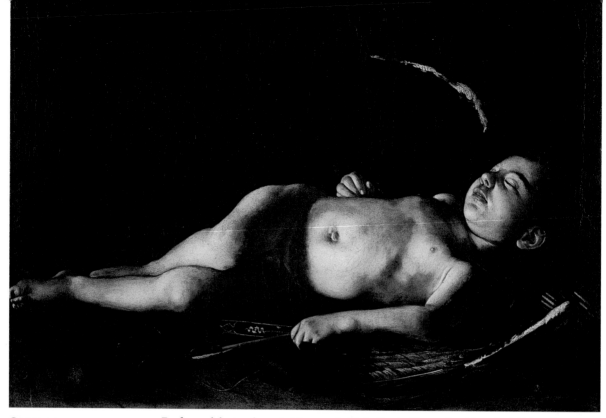

CARAVAGGIO

Sleeping Cupid

1608
Room of Jupiter's instruction

Performed during the artist's last stay in Malta for the Florentine, Niccolò dell'Antella, a member of the Order of Malta and owner of the building in piazza Santa Croce whose façade bears a frescoed reproduction of the painting, this work is an emblematic demonstration of Caravaggio's realism. Caravaggio modelled Cupid after the dead body of a child, as corroborated by recent studies. By bestowing the divine attributes of quiver and wings upon the realistic figure he rereads Olympian mythology, imparting to it the drama of terrestrial life through his gift for raw realism, revealed here at its apex.

**RAPHAEL
(RAFFAELLO SANZIO)**

Portrait of Tommaso Inghirami ("Fedra")

circa 1510
Room of Saturn

The nobleman Tommaso Inghirami from Volterra was an intimate friend of Pope Leo X, the two having grown up together at the court of Lorenzo il Magnifico. He became prefect of the Vatican Library on July 17th 1510, the likely occasion for this portrait, as also confirmed by stylistic elements. In fact, in comparison with Raphael's portraits from the preceding, Florentine period, here the artist confers an innovative monumental expression to the scholar's half bust. In a pose that echoes those of the evangelists, he seems to look for inspiration, gaze turned upward to mask the strabismus. Moreover, the realism imparts great vividness and a penetrating psychological study of the character of "Fedra" – a nickname with which Inghirami was dubbed because of the role he played in Seneca's *Hippolyta*.

**RAPHAEL
(RAFFAELLO SANZIO)**

*Madonna and Child
("Madonna del
granduca")*
circa 1506
Saturn Room

Painted during Raphael's Florentine stay, the artist had clearly well absorbed the lessons of da Vinci when he did this Madonna, who, together with Child Jesus, emerges from the dark background in a cogent compositional and chromatic simplicity sustained by his precise drawing, the legacy of his training in Perugia. Historical references to this work are lacking up to the end of the 18th Century, when it was acquired by Ferdinando III in exile in Vienna during Napoleon's interregnum. The Lorraine grand duke treasured it always (hence its name), guarding it in his private apartments. The picture was however originally destined for private purposes, as testified to by its dimensions and iconography, and recently corroborated by x-ray studies for its restoration, which have revealed a domestic scene with a window on the right leading to the exterior.

RAPHAEL (RAFFAELLO SANZIO)
*Portrait of Agnolo Doni and
Portrait of Maddalena Doni*
circa 1505-1506
Saturn Room

In 1503 the aristocrat Maddalena Strozzi married Agnolo Doni, the wealthy Florentine merchant. Later the couple turned to Michelangelo for a tondo of the *Sacred family*, the one now in the Uffizi which still bears their name (p. 26), and to Raphael for these portraits. The artist performed Maddalena's first and, as evidenced by radiographs, evidently had second thoughts about its original setting – in an interior. In fact, he later painted the background over with the current airy landscape – after the example of the diptych of the *Dukes of Urbino* by Piero della Francesca now in the Uffizi (p. 17) – so as to confer visual unity with Agnolo's portrait. The landscape is redolent of his maestro, Perugino, though it includes the more 'modern' precepts of Fra Bartolomeo, while Maddalena's pose clearly recalls da Vinci's *Mona Lisa*. Lastly, the ostentatious jewels and rich clothes donned by the couple in demonstration of their social position has been rendered with wholly Flemish precision. Two episodes from the myth of Deucalion and Pyrrhas, evident allusion to the couples hoped-for fertility, are painted in black and white on the panel's backs, the work of Maestro di Serumido.

Rear of *Portrait of Agnolo Doni*, Maestro di Serumido, *The Flood* (from the myth of Deucalion and Pyrrhas)

Rear of *Portrait of Maddalena Doni*, Maestro di Serumido, *The Rebirth of Mankind* (from the myth of Deucalion and Pyrrhas)

RAPHAEL (RAFFAELLO SANZIO)
Madonna and Child with saints ("Madonna del Baldacchino")
circa 1508
Saturn Room

This altar piece, incomplete upon Raphael's departure for Rome in 1508, was commissioned by the Dei family for the altar of their chapel in the church of Santo Spirito, where it was however never placed (the del Rosso altarpiece would instead be set there (p. 115) and later replaced by a copy). At the end of the 17th Century it was acquired by prince Ferdinando de' Medici and then, for the sake of symmetry and proportion within the Medici (picture gallery), was enlarged by Niccolò Cassana, who painted the canopy's (i.e. baldacchino) upper portion and the niche's lacunar vault. The sacred conversation takes place in an innovative spatiality that goes beyond fifteenth-century schemes: the monumental saints, in fact, are set in perspective at different depths around the throne framed by the grandiose architectural rendition. Saint Augustine, in the forefront on the right, beckons the observer to participate in the holy event.

PERUGINO
Lamentation
1495
Saturn Room

Serene composure infuses the group crowding around Christ deposed on the stone step, where Perugino's signature and the picture's date (1495) are found. Painted for the convent of Santa Chiara in Florence, there is nothing dramatic in this painting or the variations in movement of its characters. The spatial opening onto the landscape in the background underscores the lyric intonation of this *Lamentation*, an example to which Raphael would aspire when he painted the *Deposition* for Atalanta Baglioni, now in the Borghese Gallery in Rome.

RAPHAEL (RAFFAELLO SANZIO)
Madonna and Child and san Giovannino
("Madonna della seggiola")
circa 1516
Saturn Room

This is Raphael's only tondo in the Florentine tradition and perhaps one of his most famous works. The sacred group of the Madonna and Child, together with the young Saint John, is depicted with such naturalness that one forgets the complexity of the composition. It is the embrace of mother and child in affectionate intimacy – a closeness, at once sentimental and compositional, which is also emphasised by the distribution of colours: the cold tones towards the borders, the warmer ones near the centre. The perfect harmony and ample forms, clearly influenced by Michelangelo, set the painting in the artist's full-blown Roman period. Regarding the work's origins, though historical documents have remained silent, several elements point to a commission for a cultured and refined personage: the silk scarf worn as a turban in the oriental manner, so wide-spread amongst the Italian nobility, and in particular, the seat (i.e. seggiola), an elegant chair in use at the papal court, has lead to conjecturing Pope Leo X (p. 28) as the work's likely patron.

RAPHAEL (RAFFAELLO SANZIO)
Portrait of a young woman
("La Velata")
circa 1516
Jupiter Room

The image that remains impressed in the memory of whosoever sets eyes upon this masterpiece benefits nothings from knowing the name of the model who posed for it. Nonetheless, it was likely the same woman who sat for the *Madonna Sistina* in Dresden. To the memory of this face, the intense gaze and the delicate hair collected beneath the veil falling to her shoulders, here Raphael adds the rich dress with tightly fitted bodice and the slit sleeve lined with gilded silk. Raphael, living in Rome since 1508, was engaged in frescoing the Vatican Stanze, a stirring experience which likely prompted him to create this work, datable to about 1516. The pictorial richness, refined balance of the browns, golds and white, the courtly majesty of the figure and the irrepressible vitality of the dress make it one of the artist's most memorable masterpieces.

GIORGIONE
Three ages of man
circa 1500
Jupiter Room

Restoration of this painting seems to have provided confirmation of its being an early work by Giorgione. The artist was evidently influenced by Giovanni Bellini and Leonardo da Vinci, who was in Venice in 1500. The three men emerge from the dark background and are engaged in a singing lesson such as those held in the Venetian humanist circles frequented by the painter, a well-known lover of poetry and music. Such a facile reading, however, may obscure deeper meanings in the painting, hidden except to a man of the Renaissance. The work belonged to the noble Venetian family of the Vendramin and was acquired in 1698 by prince Ferdinando de' Medici.

PETER PAUL RUBENS
The four philosophers
1611-1612
Mars Room

The eldest of these philosophers, in the centre, is the Dutch humanist, Juste Lipsius, dressed in fur; at either side are his pupils, Jean de' Wouwère, whose dog is seeking attention, and Philip Rubens, the painter's brother, behind whom Rubens has add a portrait of himself, standing. The bust of Seneca, acquired by Rubens in 1605 in Rome – which he recalls here through the Palatine hill in the background – has led to a rather stoic interpretation of the painting, according to which it intends to extol the virtue of morality against the vices of time. The tulips in the vase, two opening, two still closed, allude to the characters, as at the time of its painting in 1611, Lipsius and Philip had already died. The warm tones, set off by the red curtain on the left and the carpet on the table, are evocative of the studies Rubens performed on Venetian painting while in Italy.

ANTONIE VAN DYCK
Portrait of cardinal Bentivoglio
circa 1625
Mars Room

Guido Bentivoglio, the papal liaison to Flanders, is portrayed here full-length and life-sized in a triumphant symphony of red (the colour of the cardinalship). Van Dyck, Rubens' student, paints a sumptuous picture that was received with great praise in Rome. In fact, to the realism typical of the Flemish tradition, he unites a fluid touch stemming from his knowledge of Venetian painting. The figure of the cardinal stands out from the backdrop – almost as if on stage – aided by the strip of open landscape between the column and the silken drapery. Van Dyck masterfully renders the noble lines and tapered hands of this cultured and refined man, artificer of the *War of Flanders*, whose company was sought out by four different pontiffs.

113

TITIAN (TIZIANO VECELLIO)
Mary Magdalene
circa 1535
Apollo Room

Titian's signature is visible on the pot of ointment to Magdalene's right. This is not the only time that artist depicts *Penitent Magdalene*, though in the later versions he adds a book, allusion to meditation, and a skull and crossbones to mitigate the overt sensuality of this work after the council of Trento. Datable to around 1535, it reached Florence from Urbino in 1631 with the inheritance of the Rovere family, through the marriage of its last descendant Vittoria to Ferdinando II de' Medici. The beauty of the nude unveiled beneath the flowing mane of hair, gilded by the warm lighting, is very earthy, though the eyes, still damp from weeping, are raised to the heavens, imploring pardon. Thus, the Biblical courtesan, who in house of the Pharisee washes Christ's feet with her tears, dries them with her hair and perfumed them with ointment, becomes the redeemed sinner epitomised.

TITIAN (TIZIANO VECELLIO)
Portrait of a man ("The grey-eyed man" or "The Englishman")
1545
Apollo Room

This is a portrait by Titian in his mature years, who offers up the likeness of a young man of unknown identity. The subject was certainly of the upper class, dressed in black suit, with gold chain at the neck and gloves in his right hand. The dimensions of the painting also denote an elevated social position. His penetrating look and slightly haughty air earned him the appellations given him by the romantic ambience of the time, by which the painting is still know today. Its most highly praised aspects are the acute psychological study and, above all, the chromatic blending of the black and grey tones, which serve to make the face stand out from the background.

ANDREA DEL SARTO

Lamentation ("Pietà di Luco")
1523-1524
Apollo Room

When, in order to escape the plague of 1523, Andrea del Sarto took refuge in Mugello at the Camaldolite monastery of Luco, the abbess asked him to paint a panel for the high altar of the church of San Pietro. The artist took inspiration from the *Lamentation* painted by Fra Bartolomeo nearly a decade prior (now in the Jupiter Room) for the solemn composition and the postures of Saints Peter and Paul standing behind the group. The painting's figures, on the other hand, all have a statue-like quality reminiscent of Michelangelo and Raphael. In comparison to Fra Bartolomeo's inspiring work and the other *Pietà* by Perugino (p. 111), del Sarto's rendition appears far more modern in its quick and sure brush strokes, especially in the landscape and radiant polychromatics.

ROSSO FIORENTINO

Madonna and Child with saints ("Pala Dei")
1522
Apollo Room

This altarpiece was commissioned in 1522 to Rosso Fiorentino by the Dei family for the altar of their chapel in the church of Santo Spirito. The *Madonna del Baldacchino* destined for that site had been left incomplete by Raphael when he departed for Rome (p. 111). When, in the late 17th Century, the panel entered into the possession of the Medici and was replaced in the church by a copy, it was enlarged in order make it fit an opulent Baroque frame. In the process many of the relationships in the tight composition were altered. If in fact, the artist succumbed to the wishes of his patrons to follow the illustrious iconographic model of Raphael in choosing the saints' figures, he added many others, resulting in a crowded group, seemingly compressed into the narrow space of the false architecture. Vasari writes that "it was viewed as an eccentric piece for the cleverness of the figures and abstractness of the postures." The drapes' vibrant iridescence and the figures' uneasy physiognomies are typical of Rosso Fiorentino, an artist belonging to the new generation, by now far removed from the classicism of Raphael.

ANTONIO CANOVA

Venere Italica
1810-1812
Venus Room

Toward the end of 1802, Ludwig I of the Bourbons, King of Etruria, expressed to Canova, Italy's greatest neo-classic sculptor, his desire to replace the *Medici Venus* the French had removed from the Gallery of the Uffizi. This enterprise, fraught with patriotic connotations, heightened as well by the attributes associated to this goddess, was completed by the sculptor only in 1812, and the result placed in the Uffizi. In the meantime, the new sovereign, Elisa Baciocchi, had convinced her brother, Napoleon to pay Canova the agreed upon sum of 25,000 francs. Upon the return of the original statue in 1815, Canova's Venus was transferred to Pitti Palace. Celebrated since its appearance, the goddess of love, inspired by classical models, is surprised in the act of drying herself in graceful and sensual movement. Canova shows extraordinary ability in his treatment of the cloth that Venus holds to her elegant, smooth-contoured body.

TITIAN (TIZIANO VECELLIO)
Portrait of Pietro Aretino
1545
Venus Room

Titian portrays the famous literate and libeller, Pietro Aretino, already in middle age, with full-beard and head turned resolutely leftward, a gesture that together with the expression on his face, clearly reveals the impetuousness of his character. Talented, but restless and violent, Aretino was very much dreaded by the authorities of the time because of his extraordinary *vis polemic*, which often flowed forth in verbal insult, at times reaping him substantial benefit and favours through blackmail and threats. Refined art critic, Aretino settled in Venice, where he befriended the artist, who portrayed him in a painting with bold broad strokes, harnessing all the force of his character. Yet Aretino did not like the painting, and although praising its extraordinary vitality, was perhaps perplexed by the use of a technique too innovative for the time, attributing instead the result to hasty execution. Accordingly, the writer sent the painting to grand duke Cosimo I, managing as well, through adept and insistent appeals, to garner himself a substantial sum.

TITIAN
(TIZIANO VECELLIO)
The concert
1510-1512
Venus Room

The painting, which at first had been thought the work of Giorgione, is now unanimously attributed to the young Titian: in fact, the rich *impasto* animated by the brilliant light tones are typical of Titian. The theme is music, as in the painting by Giorgione (p. 113). In fact, it originates from the same ambience, early 16th-century Venice, that held the musical arts to be fundamental in the education of the young gentleman. The three musicians emerge from the dark background with energetic plasticity: a slightly rearward chorister in feathered hat, the spinet player positioned boldly at the forefront, looking backwards toward the monk with viola in hand.

117

Modern Art Gallery

Today the Modern Art Gallery is housed on the second floor of Pitti Palace. Its history begins in about 1784, when Pietro Leopoldo of Lorraine decided to reform the Florentine academy, establishing in its interior a Modern Art Gallery for display of the artwork that received awards in academic competitions. In those same years, due to the need to decorate Pitti Palace, works of art were being collecting by order of the grand duke. By the middle of the 19th century, they were already so numerous that it was necessary to transfer many of them to the Crocetta Palace, which was thus destined, in these early years, to become the new modern art museum. After the expulsion of the Lorraine in 1859, the unification government wished to provide an official home for the grand duke's art collections, and in concomitance with the reform of the Accademia in 1867, all the works were thus brought together in the Modern Gallery of the

Academy, as the new institute came to be called. The House of Savoy, especially Vittorio Emanuele II, also added much to the collections through their acquisitions. Even the Florence City Council began a policy of acquisitions, amongst which, in 1897, the collection of *macchiaioli* paintings that had belonged to Diego Martelli. It was then that the idea was advanced of uniting the city's modern art collections under one roof. Thus, in 1914 the Italian State and the Florence City Council reached an agreement on the administration of the nascent Modern Art Gallery, which was set up in Pitti Palace in 1922, when the royal family vacated the second-floor apartments. The rooms, which have preserved their Lorraine arrangements, except for the three ceilings decorated at the time of Ferdinando II de' Medici, are made up of: the "Archduchess' Quarters" on the façade, the "New Quarter" on the courtyard up to the Ballroom, leading into the "Bourbon Quarter".

PIETRO TENERANI

Abandoned Psyche
1816-1817
Room I

Melancholy and exhausted, *Psyche* meditates after being abandoned by Love, who had caught her violating the will of the gods by observing his likeness. The subject is part of a Roman fable narrated in the *Metamorphosis* by Lucius Apuleius. The work was praised by Bertel Thorwaldsen, the Danish sculptor with whom Tenerani lived for a long time after winning the *pensionato* in Rome and frequenting the studio of Antonio Canova, an event celebrated in a speech by Pietro Giordani. The sculpture, presented at the Roman Campidoglio in 1819, was received with such enthusiasm that he duplicated it a number of times with slight variations. This sculpture belonged to Carlotta Medici Lenzoni, at whose house it came to be admired by Giovan Battista Niccolini, Giacomo Leopardi and Lorenzo Bartolini. Although neo-classical in composition, the delicacy of the limbs and smoothness of the marble, which the sculptor attained working at times by candlelight, reveal an inclination towards the natural grace and tense realism that would be the hallmark of Purism, to which Tenerani later adhered.

Antonio Canova
Calliope
1812
Room 2

Signed and dated at the base of the neck, this idealised head was commissioned to Canova by the Pisan scholar Giovanni Rosini, the neo-classical sculptor's biographer. Self-absorbed muse of epic poetry, Calliope's oval face is framed by ribbon-bound curls, the small mouth just hinting at an enigmatic smile. It is a greatly refined ideal portrait, cut in the classical tradition in the downward slope of her shoulders.

Giuseppe Bezzuoli
Carlo VIII entering Florence
1827-1829
Room 5

This large painting, performed on commission to the grand duke in 1827, was finished in 1829. It was considered a paradigm of the emerging historical genre painting, which called for representing the great themes of the past by following the grand examples of 16th and 17th-century painting, deemed the most appropriate for expressing human passions and sublime ideals. The painting shows the characters donning 17th-century costumes before Porta San Frediano in Florence. In the histrionic representation Bezzuoli however indulges in some political suggestions – for example, in representing the distress and anger of some of the onlookers – as well as to some vague nationalist allusions, such as the group at the right depicting the opponents of imperial power, such as Macchiavelli, Capponi and Savonarola.

SILVESTRO LEGA
The starling's song
1867
Room 12

Exhibited for the first time at the 'Florentine Promotrice' in 1867, where it received critical acclaim, The starling's song represents one of Silvestro Lega's greatest artistic achievements. The serene atmosphere of the intimate domestic scene is counterpointed by the figures' formal postures, evidently inspired by 15th-century Tuscan painters, most notably Piero della Francesca. Adding to the scene's idyllic atmosphere is the swatch of gentle Tuscan landscape visible through the window, the light from which suffuses the young women gathered round the piano. The woman seated at the piano is Virginia Battelli, with whom the artist spent one of his most fertile periods at the Battelli family villa, in a atmosphere similar to this painting, most certainly conducive to artistic inspiration.

ANTONIO CISERI
Ecce Homo
1871-1891
Room 14

This painting, portraying Jesus presented to the crowd by Pontius Pilate, originates from an 1871 government commission. Its gestation was a long one and at its appearance after the painter's death in 1891, it was generally praised, even by those such as Diego Martelli, who were not at all well disposed towards the academic trend of which Ciseri had become an outstanding representative. However, the art critic and collector appreciated the painting's lighting effects and transparent tones of white that likened the work to the most modern pictorial experiences. From the outset, the picture elicited surprise, due to the psychological study of the characters: Pilate's wife, for instance, is rendered quite conspicuously, probably suggested to the painter by literary sources narrating the woman's sincere concern for Christ's fate and her efforts to stay her husband's misguided course of action. Although tense and highly dramatic, the work is nevertheless not unlike the paintings of the time that depicted touching human events within monumental archaeological reconstructions, thereby anticipating the aesthetic solutions which Alma Tadema would champion. The canvas is located in one of the three rooms that bear the original decorations from the time of Ferdinando II de' Medici (the other two follow in sequence).

GIOVANNI FATTORI
The Palmieri rotunda
1866
Room 18

Painted in 1866, this small painting represents the rotunda of the well-known Leghorn bath houses, where some ladies engaging in quiet conversation are set in relief against the coloured tarsia in the background, caught between the intense blue of the sea and the clear bright sky whose light tinges the shade of the tent. Moreover, the scalloped border of the tent provides a sense of breadth and depth to the scene, whose fulcrum is the group of figures clustered towards the centre. A masterpiece of *macchiaiolo* painting, the work testifies to the technique aimed at reproducing the impression of reality through the study of chromatic matching: the blending of "macchie" (splotches) of colour-light and colour-shade, and consequently the forsaking of the *chiaroscuro* technique.

Boboli Gardens

The Boboli Garden complex gets its name from the medieval toponym for the area in which it is located. It is a splendid example of the consummate Italian garden and, despite the modifications it has undergone over the centuries, has maintained its original formulation, as conceived of in the mid-16th Century by its first inventor, Niccolò Pericoli, known as 'il Tribolo', favoured artist of Cosimo I. Although after Tribolo's death supervision of the work passed on to a succession of eminent personalities, such as Giorgio Vasari – who first designed the Grotta Grande, which was later modified by Bernardo Buontalenti to give it is current form – and Bartolomeo Ammannati, the overall effect is very much in keeping with Tribolo's fundamental idea: the strict bond between the garden and the palace it surrounded, of which the amphitheatre was an idealised extension, echoing the courtyard by Ammannati. In the early 17th Century the garden was enlarged, mostly the work of Giulio Parigi, who designed the theatrical layout of the Island Pond. After the Medici dynasty came to a close in 1737, a period of decadence ensued, but between 1765 and 1790, under the Lorraine government, important restorations were undertaken and buildings added, such as the Kaffeehaus and Lemon House. Finally, in the 19th Century, the splendid new entranceway, called the "Annalena gate", was created, though it was in this same century that the original plant labyrinths were destroyed, perhaps the most traumatic event in the history of this garden of wonders. With its statues, rich vegetation and monumental fountains, Boboli Gardens extend before our fascinated eyes – a true open-air museum.

Anfiteatro

Ideal extension of the building's courtyard, the wide Amphitheatre was built by Alfonso Parigi between 1630 and 1634, and inaugurated in 1637 on the occasion of the coronation of the grand duchess of Tuscany, Vittoria della Rovere, wife of Ferdinando II, with a choreographic succession inspired by Tasso's *Jerusalem Delivered*. At the time, the tiered steps were actually terraces on which various tree species were planted, and the balustrade running the entire length of perimeter at the top held aedicules containing statues, for the most part classical. It was Joseph Cacialli who in 1818 transformed the original amphitheatre into the current masonry structure with its arrangement of statues alternating with terracotta urns painted to resemble marble. In the amphitheatre's centre are found an Egyptian obelisk from Luxor, Egypt dating back to 1500 BC, and an ancient granite tub originally from the Thermal Baths of Caracalla, both brought here from the garden of Villa Medici in Rome.

Vasca del Forcone

Between 1777 and 1778, Zanobi del Rosso transformed the original, rectangular collecting basin from the aqueduct of Arcetri into the basin we see today, called "Vasca del Forcone" (basin of the great fork), because of the sculptural group set in its centre in 1635. The bronze statue of *Neptune*, done by Stoldo Lorenzi between 1565 and 1568 for a nearby garden no longer in existence, depicts the god of the seas brandishing his trident over a rock cliff, below which some sea divinities are crouching. Beyond the Basin extend semicircular terraces on top of which in the back is the large statue of *Plenty*, begun by Giambologna in 1608 and completed by Pietro Tacca and Sebastiano Salvini between 1636 and 1637. This allegorical statue is a portrait of Johanna of Austria, wife of the grand duke Francesco I.

Giardino del Cavaliere

The Giardino del Cavaliere (Knight's Garden) takes its name from the rampart known as the "Bastion of Malatesta the Knight", designed by Michelangelo in 1529. One enters from the scenic stairway designed by Giuseppe del Rosso in 1792, whose lower-most portion is flanked by two *Muses* (Roman copies of Greek originals). The medicinal plants originally cultivated here were replaced by exotic varieties in 1612, when the garden was remodelled after a design by Giulio Parigi. In that same year the Knight's Lodge (Casino del Cavaliere) was built. This is a large room originally used as a storeroom for pots, but subsequently utilised by Cardinal Leopoldo de' Medici as a meeting place for scholars and scientists, and then enlarged by Cosimo III for his son, Gian Gastone. Today it houses the Porcelain Museum (Museo delle Porcelane), where sumptuous Italian, French, German and Viennese ceramics are displayed. In the garden's centre is the Fountain of Monkeys (Fontana delle Scimmie), so called because of the two 17th-century bronze monkeys from the school of Pietro Tacca at the feet of the shaft sustaining the bowl, on which rests a sixteenth-century marble putto, thought to be by either Stoldo Lorenzi or Pierino da Vinci.

Vasca dell'Isola

The large pond is dominated by the fountain in its central island. Access to the island is through two gates upheld by paired columns topped by marble *Capricorns*, symbolising Cosimo I de' Medici. The Fountain of Oceanus was fashioned in 1576 by Giambologna for the lawn of the amphitheatre and moved to the centre of the pond in 1636. The allegorical statue, *Oceanus*, a copy by Raffaello Romanelli of the original now held in the Bargello Museum, rises above a pedestal, about which are arranged the *Nile*, *Ganges* and *Euphrates* Rivers. The pedestal is adorned with sculpted bas-reliefs depicting mythological scenes. The fountain's bowl was made from a single granite block, transported from the Island of Elba by order of Cosimo I and sculpted by Tribolo in 1550. Immersed in the pond's waters are *Perseus on horseback* and *Andromeda*, both by Giovan Battista Pieratti. This same artist, together with his brother Domenico, Cosimo Salvestrini and Francesco Susini executed the two Fountains of Cupid on the northern and southern sides of the pond, while the Fountains of the Harpies, bordering the eastern and western sides, were sculpted in the 18th Century by Innocenzo Spinazzi after 17th-century originals. The espaliers delimiting the space around the Basin bear niches holding statues from the Florentine school of the 17th Century.

Grotta di Annalena

During the work of enlarging the garden entrance in via Romana, in 1817 the architect Giuseppe Cacialli created the Annalena Grotto, within whose interior was set the sculptural group of *Adam and Eve* by Michelangelo Naccherino (1616) which had previously been kept in one of the hanging gardens then plentiful at Boboli. This noteworthy

sculpture finds a perfect setting within the Annalena Grotto, an environment echoing Bernardo Buontalenti's Grand Grotto, especially in the decorative sponges and large masks (*mascheroni*). These latter, fashioned in white marble by Ottaviano Giovannozzi following the design of Cacialli, stand out conspicuously from the warm colours of the sponges. The decoration is completed by shells and decorative elements that simulate a cavern's natural stratification and the striking ceiling with decorations representing the attributes of Poseidon on an ultramarine background.

Grotta del Buontalenti
(Grotta Grande)

Buontalenti's Grotto is located on the northern side of the Square of Bacchus (Piazzale di Bacco), at the end of the passageway built by Vasari to unite Pitti Palace with Palazzo Vecchio (p. 126). In fact, it was Giorgio Vasari, the architect and painter from Arezzo, who between 1556 and 1560 designed and executed the core of this suggestive complex, originally a plant nursery. The façade was created beside the entranceway loggia, and the niches on either side filled with Baccio Bandinelli's statues of *Ceres* and *Apollo*. Subsequently, between 1583 and 1593, the nursery was transformed into a grotto, according to the design of Bernardo Buontalenti, thus giving rise to one of the most fascinating places in the gardens. Divided into three areas, the first once housed Michelangelo's *Prisoners* (p. 33-34), replaced with cast copies in 1924. This room is decorated by bas-reliefs in spongy material and frescoes by Bernardino Poccetti. Here, water once gushed forth from encrustations throughout the walls, creating a spectacular effect as the wet materials glistened in all their chromatic glory. The marble group placed in the second room in 1587 is the work of Vincenzo de' Rossi and probably represents *Theseus and Helen*, but could also represent Anchises and Venus or Aeneas and Dido, in any event, couples linked to myths surrounding Italy's origins. Finally, in the centre of the innermost room is the fountain of *Venus* that owes its name to the masterpiece sculpted by Giambologna in 1573.

Grotta Grande, interior view of first room

Giambologna, *Venus*, 1573

Bernardino Poccetti, frescoed ceiling of Grotta Grande

PALAZZO VECCHIO

Linked from its origins to the vicissitudes of the city government, Palazzo Vecchio was built between 1299 and 1315 with the purpose of providing a new and fitting location to the Priori. In fact, after the defeat of the Ghibellini (supporters of the Emperor) and the emergence of the new social classes, the administration of the city was conducted by the Gonfaloniere, together with the Trade Guilds, of which the Priori was the most powerful. The building, planned by Arnolfo di Cambio, was actually erected upon the ruins of the homes of the Uberti family, supporters of the Ghibellini faction. Originally, it was a simple box structure in rusticated ashlar, with a necessarily asymmetrical tower, as it was erected upon the pre-existing Foraboschi Tower. Even then, the open courtyard was overlooked by the Arms Chamber, the only area of the palace that still maintains its original aspect today, while the upper floor is where the High Council met in the Sala dei Dugento. Over the centuries, the building has been modified a number of times to suit the needs of the city rulers, and its name changed accordingly as well: during he 15th Century, the Medici had Michelozzo restructure the courtyard of the then Palazzo della Signoria, while Benedetto and Giuliano da Maiano made alterations to the Sala dei Dugento. After the death of Lorenzo il Magnifico in 1492 and the ousting of the Medici, in 1495 the new republican government enlarged the building on the eastern side with the addition of the room of the High Council, thus destined to become the Salone dei Cinquecento. In 1540, Cosimo I de' Medici rose to power, and moved the court residence to the Palace. Later, the Medici court was transferred to Pitti Palace, hence the former ducal residence became known by its present-day appellative the "Old Palace", parts of which still house the Mayor's offices, Town Council and other city offices.

Courtyard

The building's courtyard owes its current appearance to the work of Giorgio Vasari in 1565, on the occasion of the wedding of Francesco de' Medici to Johanna of Austria. His design – a grand commemorative scheme in keeping with the progressive adaptation of the austere republican building to the demands of court – called for adding the plaster decorations on the columns, the grotesques and the frescoes depicting the cities of the Habsburg empire that decorate the vault and walls. In those same years, Francesco del Tadda and Raffaello di Domenico di Polo sculpted the fountain now in the courtyard's centre, though the design was also Vasari's. The *Putto holding a dolphin* within the fountain was originally by Verrocchio, today replaced by a copy on display in the building's interior. The courtyard was reconstructed and enlarged in 1454 according to Renaissance canons by Michelozzo, who established a new architectural order by modifying the colonnade, opening a new tier of windows and adding decorations in graffito ashlar with gold lilies, of which some traces still remain.

Sala dei Dugento
First floor

The "Hall of the Two Hundred" is linked to the building's origins, in that reunions of the old Council of the People were held here in the presence of the powerful Priori and Gonfaloniere. Even today it is the venue for town council meetings, and therefore cannot usually be visited. It was restructured by Benedetto and Giuliano da Maiano who, with other collaborators, sculpted the lacunar ceiling – decorated with lilies and roses – and the friezes adorned by garlands and the coats of arms of the Florentine People.

Salone dei Cinquecento
First floor

The large "Hall of the Five Hundred" originated during the republican era, when, as advocated by Savonarola, representation in the city council was widened to a much larger segment of the population (after the example of the Venetian Republic). Consequently, the Sala dei Dugento was no longer large enough to conduct the council meetings. Designed by Cronaca and built between 1494 and 1496, it however owes his current arrangement to Cosimo I who, as elected duke, wished to transform it into a meeting room pervaded by symbols of his own power and glory. The commemorative program was begun in 1542-1543 by Baccio Bandinelli and Baccio d'Agnolo, who created the Udienza, that is, the elevated tribuna at the hall's northern end that once held the ducal throne. Its architecture aspires to that of a Roman triumphal arch, decorated with statues by Bandinelli, Vincenzo de' Rossi and Giovan Battista Caccini. Modification of the hall to suit the duke's wishes then continued under the guidance of Giorgio Vasari. In 1503, the Gonfaloniere Pier Soderini commissioned da Vinci and Michelangelo to perform frescoes depicting the battles of Anghiari and Cascina. These were however never completed, and the walls now bear representations of the victories of Cosimo I over Siena and Pisa, done by Vasari himself and others from his workshop (1567-1571). On the ceiling, raised once again by about seven meters between 1563 and 1565, Vasari unfolds his stately iconographic design centred on the apotheosis of Cosimo I and flanked by sections bearing allegorical and historical representations. The hall also contains Michelangelo's sculptural group, *Victory*, sculpted in 1533-1534 for the tomb of Pope Julius II. The masterpiece was however never used and was eventually donated by Michelangelo's nephew, Leonardo Buonarroti, to Cosimo I, who had it placed here as a symbol of his conquest of Siena.

Studiolo of Francesco I
First floor

The relationship of Art to Nature is the underlying theme of the rich decoration of the Studiolo, or study of grand duke Francesco I. The small room opens like a precious jewel case in the wall of Salone dei Cinquecento, thanks to a passageway added in the 19th Century. Created by Francesco I de' Medici, who succeeded his father, Cosimo I in 1564, it is testament to Francesco's character: inclined to a life of meditation and the study of science and philosophy, rather than to the drudgeries of government. Thus, in 1570 the duke entrusted Giorgio Vasari with creating a place where he would be able to study and safeguard his collection of minerals, precious gems and rare articles. The artist, aided by the court scholar, Vincenzo Borghini, produced a decorative design centred on the allegorical representation of the natural elements and man's efforts to transform them, thus creating one of the most cogent testimonies to the cultural climate of the time. The vault fresco is dominated by the figure of *Prometheus*, surrounded by the four *Elements*, armoire-panel paintings were put on the walls, and bronze statues in the niches. The charming Studiolo is the result of the contributions of many other artists, such as the painters Santi di Tito and Alessandro Allori and sculptors Giambologna and Bartolomeo Ammannati, to name only a few.

Chapel of Eleonora
Second floor
Quarter of Eleonora

When in 1540 Cosimo I de' Medici took residence in Palazzo della Signoria, he reserved the second floor quarters for his consort, Eleonora of Toledo, and had them completely remodelled by the architect Battista del Tasso to suit the needs of the duchess and her entourage. One enters the Chapel of Eleonora from the Green Room, through the marble door designed by Bartolomeo Ammannati. Between 1540 and 1545 the chapel was elegantly frescoed throughout by Agnolo Bronzino, painter in the graces of the ducal family who performed some of his most celebrated work here. The symbol of the Trinity on the ceiling is crowned by *Penitent Saint Jerome*, *Saint John the Evangelist*, *Saint Michael the Archangel vanquishing Satan*, and *Saint Francis*, *in the act of receiving the stigmata*. The rich and luminous decoration continues on the walls, where biblical episodes related to Moses are depicted. On the back wall, placed between the paintings of the *Announcing Angel* and *Maria Annunciata*, is the *Deposition of Christ*, repainted by Bronzino himself to replace the original which Cosimo I had given as a gift to Emperor Charles V's keeper of the seals, now in the museum of Besançon.

Sala dell'Udienza
Second floor

In 1472 the Signoria decided to divide the large second-floor Great Hall above the Sala dei Dugento. The Sala dell'Udienza (Hearing room) was therefore obtained and given over to the administration of justice. The complicated restructuring was carried out by Benedetto da Maiano, who erected the partition wall and, together with his brother, Giuliano, executed the beautiful marble tranceway surmounted by a statue of *Justice*. Giuliano and co-workers also performed the richly decorated coffered ceiling and inlaid door leaves, while the other marble door leading into the Chapel of the Priori is the work of Baccio d'Agnolo. Later, Cosimo I used it as a hearing room, where seated on a canopied throne he would give audience. In the 1543 the duke entrusted Francesco Salviati with frescoing the walls with the history of Furio Camillo, the general who saved Rome from the invasion of the Gauls. The painter, trained in Rome, depicted grandiose triumphal scenes alternating with allegorical figures, clear allusions to Cosimo's rise to power and the splendour of his rein.

Sala dei Gigli
Second floor

The other area obtained in 1472 by dividing the fourteenth-century Great Hall is the Sala dei Gigli (Room of Lilies), which has preserved its fifteenth-century appearance intact. The room walls are decorated in gold lilies on a blue background, in honour of the Angiò, protectors of the Guelph faction. The same motif covers the ceiling by Giuliano da Maiano, who also executed the frieze and, together with his brother, Benedetto, the portal leading into the Hearing Room. Between 1482 and 1485, Domenico Ghirlandaio painted the great fresco on the wall opposite the entrance. The representation of enthroned *San Zanobius between Saints Stephan and Lawrence* with famous personages of ancient Rome is redolent of the humanistic ideals that blended religiousness and civil commitment. The room holds several masterpieces by Donatello: the bronze group with the biblical heroin, Judith, in the act of beheading King Holofernes of the Assyrians. It was originally kept in the garden of the Medici Villa in via Larga (p. 185) until being confiscated in 1494 when the Medici were deposed. It was then set before Palazzo della Signoria, where a copy remains to this day to symbolise the vanquishing of tyranny.

129

PINACOTECA DELLO SPEDALE DEGLI INNOCENTI

The rich picture gallery within the complex of the foundling hospital, Spedale degli Innocenti, holds a number of important works of art. The collection, either the original property of the hospital or acquired following the suppression of ecclesiastical institutes, is kept in the hall overlying the portico. Designed by Filippo Brunelleschi in 1419, the building is one of the most famous examples of renaissance Florentine architecture – an elegant and harmonious expression of the humanist culture and, at the same time, an important institution for the tutelage of childhood. Extending the portico along the full length of building's façade, Brunelleschi (inspired by Roman porticoed squares and medieval loggias) unites the open space of the square with the interior of the building, attaining an architecture governed by the perfectly modular repetition of cubical space. The height of the columns is in fact equal to the length of the arches' spans and the distance separating the arches from the loggia's inner wall. In 1487, Andrea della Robbia's glazed terracotta tondi depicting new-borns in swaddling clothes were placed under the nine arcades on the façade dominated by alternating white plaster and grey *pietra serena*, Brunelleschi's trademark. Brunelleschi oversaw construction of the building until 1436, when Francesco della Luna followed the hospital's progress up to its solemn inauguration on April 11, 1451.

SANDRO BOTTICELLI
Madonna and Child with angel
circa 1464-1465

This early work by Botticelli clearly originates in Filippo Lippi's *Madonna and Child with angel*, now in the Uffizi (p. 18). In fact, Botticelli received his first artistic education at Lippi's workshop. Botticelli, however, opts for a different background, replacing Lippi's open landscape with an arch with bronze and textured-marble capitals that recalls the motifs of the workshop of Verrocchio, where Botticelli continued his training. The Madonna was found in a room adjoining the church sacristy of the Spedale degli Innocenti. The room was used to receive abandoned children, a role well suited to the painting's theme of holy motherhood, rendered here with the utmost tenderness.

PIERO DI COSIMO

Enthroned Madonna and Child with angels and saints Peter, John the Evangelist, Dorothy (?) and Catherine of Alexandria
circa 1493

Child Jesus offers a ring to Saint Catherine on the right and a rose to the figure on the left, representing in all probability, Saint Dorothy. Both are "brides of Christ", the former, guardian of unmarried youth, the latter, patron saint of childbirth; thus explaining their presence in the painting found here within the Spedale degli Innocenti, an institution dedicated since its inception to aiding abandoned children. The work was commissioned by Piero del Pugliese for the altar of the family chapel in the hospital church, where it was put in 1493, surmounted by the glazed terracotta lunette by Andrea della Robbia, now in the courtyard on the left side. The naturalistic details and sharp delineation, rendered in glistening colours, reveal Piero di Cosimo's familiarity with Flemish painting. The throne has a studied structure, with a pair of flanking candelabra bearing two plump little angels, and above the arch, a black and white cherub in imitation of the sculpture.

DOMENICO GHIRLANDAIO AND BARTOLOMEO DI GIOVANNI

Adoration of the Magi
1488

The work was commissioned by Francesco di Giovanni Tesori, who had it placed on the main altar of the church at the Spedale degli Innocenti in 1488 (the date can be seen on the beams above the arch of the ancient ruins). Two lavishly dressed figures participate in the Magi's procession and represent merchants of the Silk Guild, who contributed to establishing the foundling hospital. Domenico Ghirlandaio can also be identified as the figure near the pillar on the left, who is looking toward the observer, and next to him, dressed in black, is Giovanni Tesori. Ghirlandaio was helped to execute this panel by a number of collaborators, amongst whom his brother, David, and Bartolomeo di Giovanni, who did the predella and Slaughter of the innocents in the background. This episode and the two wounded children presented by Saint John the Baptist and Saint John the Evangelist in the presence of the Virgin and Child, as if to invoke their protection, are to be viewed in strict relation to the mission of the foundling hospital. The original frame was lost when the altarpiece was dismembered.

CHURCHES

BADIA FIORENTINA

The Florentine abbey was founded in 978 as a Benedictine monastery dedicated to the Virgin Mary by Willa, the Marquise of Tuscany and mother of the Marquis of Tuscany, Ugo, who is buried here. The complex was built abutting the city walls along via del Proconsolo, in an orientation perpendicular to its current one, that is, the church façade faced west and the three apses eastwards toward the walls. In 1172 these walls were demolished to enclose the growing city in a new, wider ring. In 1285 Arnolfo di Cambio, an architect then employed in many of the city's most important projects, enlarged the church, maintaining however its orientation. Parts of this gothic structure are still visible on the apse's external wall and the upper portions of the façade (visible from the courtyard of the Pretura). He then erected the bell tower, partly destroyed by the Florentines in 1307 to punish the monks for their refusal to pay taxes, though by 1330 the two last tiers of double lancet windows and cusps had already been reconstructed. Between 1432 and 1438, Bernardo Rossellino built the cloister (Chiostro degli Aranci), which was then adorned with *Stories of Saint Benedict* by a painter identified as Giovanni di Consalvo, of Portuguese origin, as was the abbot at the time. In the early 16th Century, Giovan Battista Pandolfini entrusted Benedetto da Rovezzano with construction of his family's chapel and the porticoed atrium onto which it opens. The most radical transformation of the Abbey occurred in 1628 by the hand of architect Matteo Segaloni, who realised the church in the form of Greek cross with its façade over the arcade. At the same time, the original ceiling decorations were removed and replaced with the beautiful carved wooden ceiling.

MINO DA FIESOLE

Monument to Ugo, Marquis of Tuscany
1469-1481
Beneath the left choir

In 1469 Mino da Fiesole, who performed the sepulchral monument to Bernardo Giugni in the Abbey and the Neroni dossal, was charged by the Benedictine monks with completing the monumental tomb of Marquis Ugo. Thirty years prior, they had already given the same commission to Luca della Robbia, who however never completed more than the model. The monks wished to commemorate this illustrious personage linked to the imperial family of Otto III. In fact, Ugo had been a great benefactor of the monastery founded by his mother, Willa, in 978, so much so as to be considered its true patron. Mino da Fiesole, who had lived a period in Rome, followed the example of Bernardo Rossellino's work at Santa Croce (p. 155). The statue of Charity in the centre of the porphyry panelling that divides the background, and the tondo of the Madonna and Child were received with great praise. The monument was finished after a long hiatus in 1481. Later, during the 1629 rearrangement of the entire church, it too was moved from its original position to be set where it can still be seen today.

IN·REBVS·DVBIIS·MARIAM·COGITA·MARIAM·INVOCA

FILIPPINO LIPPI

*Apparition of the Virgin
to Saint Bernard*
1481 or 1486
To the left of the entrance

The dating of this work is uncertain due to ambiguity in the documents communicating the painting's commissioning from Filippino Lippi by Piero di Francesco del Pugliese, whose portrait in profile can be seen in its lower right portion. The Virgin, accompanied by four angels, appears to Saint Bernard, and from this mystic vision the saint draws inspiration for his writings, in which Maria is invoked to grant the strength to resist temptation. In fact, Satan in chains and an owl, the symbol of wisdom, are depicted in a cavern on the right. Above, other Trappists are shown in various monastic activities: two are intent in dialogue, two others absorbed in contemplation, while yet another comes to the aid of a needy fellow monk. A sign placed on a rock above Saint Bernard's halo bears an inscription, an erudite reference to Stoicism, of which Pugliese was an adherent: it was in fact the cardinal virtue of this philosophical current, forbearance of human tribulations, that determined the affinity Pugliese felt to the mystic saint.

135

BATTISTERO DI SAN GIOVANNI

Popular tradition has it that the Baptistery was a Roman temple devoted to Mars which was later converted to a church. Nonetheless, the building's true dating is still an open question. According to some, it is a 5th-century monument, converted between the 6th and 8th centuries, while others consider it a Romanesque construction, as testified to by the marble decoration. What is certain is that it was consecrated in 1059, dedicated to Saint John the Baptist and used for the holy sacrament of baptism as well as representing the Cathedral. The structure is octagonal and covered in 'Lunigiana' white and 'Prato' green marbles. A number of additions have been made to the original building: the attic, the pyramidal roof concealing the segmented dome, and the lantern surmounted by ball and cross, dated to 1174. The Arte di Calimala, the powerful merchants guild who were patrons of the Baptistery, commissioned the three bronze doors: the southern and oldest one by Andrea Pisano in 1336, the northern one then entrusted to Lorenzo Ghiberti, who earned the commission in a 1401 competition, and lastly, the so-called "Gates of Heaven", also by Ghiberti (p. 57). The building was inspired by classical structures, as is clear in its interior, where the walls, also done in the same traditional black and white marble facing as the exterior, are divided on the lower tier by pillars alternating with granite columns, and in the upper order by the pilasters dividing the gallery. The pavement is covered with marble intarsia, with the Zodiac and oriental-style motifs drawn from fabrics. Precious mosaics cover the dome and vault of the apse.

VENETIAN MOSAICISTS (AFTER CARTOONS BY COPPO DI MARCOVALDO, MELIORE, MAESTRO DELLA MADDALENA AND CIMABUE)

Christ amongst the Seraphs and heavenly hosts, Scenes from the Genesis, Story of Saint Joseph, Story of Christ and Story of Saint John the Baptist, the Last Judgement
circa 1270-1320
Dome

The exquisite mosaic decoration in the dome's concentric bands narrates, starting from the bottom (those most visible to the faithful): the *Stories of Saint John the Baptist*, then *Christ*, followed by his father, *Saint Joseph*, the *Genesis*, and finally, *Christ amongst the seraphic angels* with the *Celestial hierarchies*, to culminate in a velarium of plant and symbolic motifs typical of the Early Christian tradition. The three eastern segments toward the apse bear the *Last Judgement*, with the huge figure of Christ in its centre. Venetian artists specialised in this extremely costly technique, deemed the most suitable to represent the glory of God, were called upon to render the cartoons drawn by local artists, such as Coppo di Marcovaldo, author of *Christ* and *Hell*, Meliore, Maestro della Maddalena and Cimabue, to whom the first *Stories of John the Baptist* have been attributed.

MICHELOZZO AND DONATELLO

Funeral monument to the antipope John XXIII
1424-1427
To the right of the scarsella

The difficult years of the Schism, during which two popes had been elected contemporaneously, had barely terminated when Baldassare Coscia died in Florence on December 22, 1419. The antipope John XXIII, deposed the year before by the council of Constance, was honoured with a burial in the Baptistery by virtue of his intimacy with the Medici, who commissioned the tomb from Michelozzo and Donatello. The two artists collaborated on the project: the former designed it and probably sculpted the marble parts (certainly the *Virtues* in the plinth niches), while the latter fashioned the gilded bronze statue in the bier. Inserted between two columns with the sarcophagus suspended on two consoles, the funeral monument applies some gothic elements, such as the open curtain used to form a cuspidate crowning. However, renaissance elements also abound, as can be seen, for example, in the deliberate classicism of the cupids, transformed here into small angels unfurling the inscription.

DUOMO
(SANTA MARIA DEL FIORE)

It took more than a century for the Florentines to get accustomed to the name of their new cathedral, Santa Maria del Fiore, a title combining the name of Holy Mother with that of the city symbol, the red *fleur-de-lis*. They went on calling it by the name of the former Romanesque cathedral, Santa Reparata, which by end of the 14th Century had grown inadequate for the prosperous city in expansion. In 1294, Arnolfo di Cambio, the architect to whom the Florentines most ambitious projects were entrusted, was charged with raising the new cathedral where its precursor once stood. However, Cambio died only a few years later, and in 1334 the powerful Arte della Lana (Wool Guild) entrusted supervision of the work to Giotto. The work continued under Giotto, who concerned himself mainly with the bell tower which bears his name, only to be interrupted once again three years later by his death, when Andrea Pisano took over. However, it was Francesco Talenti who provided new impetus to the project, to which he also made some modifications. He managed to complete the nave and side aisles, but having reached the galleries and the octagonal drum was faced with the problem of the roof: since the times of the Pantheon no one had succeeded in vaulting a span of such vast dimensions. Filippo Brunelleschi succeeded with a revolutionary project entered in the competition held in 1418. The design called for two concentric shells, anchored to a system of ribs. The rising structure was self-bearing – the first ever to be built without the use of the traditional wooden framework to support it. In 1436 the dome was finished and Pope Eugenius IV consecrated the new cathedral, embellished with stained glass windows fashioned following the cartoons by artists such as Ghiberti, Donatello, Andrea del Castagno and Paolo Uccello. The marble lantern, set in place after Brunelleschi's death, was completed by Verrocchio with the addition of the bronze globe and cross. The façade, on the other hand, remained unfinished. Cambio had got only as far as half its projected height, which was then demolished in 1587. It was not until three centuries later, between 1871 and 1887, that the church finally had its neo-gothic façade, according to a revival of medieval archetectural styles. Over and beyond a sacred place of worship, the Duomo represented the Pantheon of the city's glories and forum for its cultural activities: it was here that Dante's *Divine Comedy* was read and the *Certame Coronario* held in defence of the Italian vernacular.

Giorgio Vasari
and Federico Zuccari

Last Judgement
1572-1574 and 1576-1579
Dome

For his dome Brunelleschi had foreseen a mosaic decoration such as that in the Baptistery. Almost a century and a half later in 1572, by will of Cosimo I, Giorgio Vasari started the fresco of the *Last Judgement*, in whose design he collaborated, as in many other enterprises, with Vincenzo Borghini. The vault was divided into four sections, more than a fifth filled with figures of the *Prophets*. In its execution Vasari clearly imitated Michelangelo's art, as his work was considered to be the incomparable paragon of perfection - the acme of the artistic parable set forth by Vasari in his *1550 Lives of the Most Eminent Painters, Sculptors, and Architects*. After his death in 1574, the decoration was brought to completion in 1579 by Federico Zuccari and collaborators. Zuccari, a painter from the Italian region of Marche who had worked in Rome and England, adopted (as Vasari before him in the area immediately under the lantern) the more rapid technique of painting on an already dry surface. He portrayed many of his contemporaries, amongst which he also added a self-portrait.

Sacristy of the Mass

In the tumult of activity leading up to the cathedral's consecration, in 1436 two supervisors of the cathedral workers were given the assignment of furnishing one of the two new sacristies. Precedence was given to the northern side, subsequently called the Sacristy of the Mass, in distinction to the Sacristy of Canons facing the ancient cloister on the south. No trace remains today of the result of that assignment. The arrangement which instead is visible today dates back to the years immediately following the consecration. The marquetry cabinets were well suited to application of the scientific principles of perspective set forth by Brunelleschi, at that time busy in completing the dome, choir and galleries. The cabinets on the southern walls (to the right) and north (to the left) were begun in 1436 by Agnolo di Lazzaro and Antonio Manetti. After a long interruption, in 1463 Giuliano da Maiano, with his brother Benedetto, continued the decoration on the east wall (opposite the entrance), where *Saint Zanobius* is represented between two disciples and the *Annunciation*, after a cartoon by Maso Finiguerra. On the entrance side, above the cabinet within a marble aedicule and lavabo by Buggiano, they depicted the *Nativity* and *Presentation*. The decoration is completed by a rose window with the *Agnus Dei*, from which originate two rows of puti with festoons. The bronze door in the sacristy is the work of Michelozzo, Maso di Bartolomeo and Luca della Robbia, this last also the author of the overlying lunette in glazed terracotta with the *Ascension*.

Paolo Uccello

Equestrian monument to John Hawkwood
1436
Left aisle, third span

Paolo Uccello was entrusted by the Opera del Duomo (the Cathedral Authority) to fresco the *Equestrian Monument to John Hawkwood* (known as Giovanni Acuto), the English condottiere engaged by the Florentines to command their army from 1377 until his death in 1394. The fact that a mercenary soldier is celebrated within a sacred place must be attributed to the cathedral's growing role as Pantheon of the city's triumphs and glory. The painter used green earthen paints to give the illusion of a bronze equestrian monument, illuminated by natural lighting from the left. Vasari judged the horse's stance, with two legs lifted on the same side, as unnatural. Paolo Uccello employed some perspective artifices, whereby he painted the table in foreshortening (reminiscent of Masaccio). Therefore, the horse, with his heavily chiaroscuro rider, were meant to be viewed from below, at a plane parallel to the viewer's. The elegant frame adorned with grotesques is a sixteenth-century work by Lorenzo di Credi. In 1443 the Opera del Duomo commissioned Paolo Uccello with designing the stained glass for the lunettes on the dome's drum, as well as with decorating the clock on the inner wall of the façade with the *Prophets*.

Andrea del Castagno

Equestrian monument to Niccolò da Tolentino
1456
Left aisle, second span

Ten years after Paolo Uccello exalted the memory of John Hawkwood, the Opera del Duomo had Andrea del Castagno immortalise the heroic deeds of Niccolò da Tolentino, the captain of fortune that led the Florentines to victory against Siena in the Battle of San Romano, an event already depicted by Paolo Uccello (p. 16). The fresco is to be observed according to rigorous perspective cannons in the classical tradition, so well assimilated by the author through his study of contemporary sculpture. Simulating a marble equestrian monument, the painter's masterful technique endows the horse and rider with amazing vividness and spry restlessness. Within these hallowed walls Castagno celebrates the wholly terrestrial virtues of a man of action.

OGNISSANTI

The gothic church and convent of Ognissanti (All Saints) were built beginning in 1251. The Benedictine order of the Umiliati settled here and made it one of the city's most burgeoning areas, thanks to their skill in the art of glasswork for churches and the dying of fabrics, which they exported throughout all Europe. The building of the church progressed quickly up to its conclusion in 1260. Numerous works of art were commissioned from the most important painters of the 14th Century: Giotto, author of the *Maestà* now in the Uffizi (p. 12), his student Taddeo Gaddi, whose beautiful fresco of the Crucifixion remains in the sacristy; as well as artists of the 15th Century, such as Ghirlandaio and Botticelli. In 1561 the order, by now reduced in number and in moral decline, were forced to move and were replaced by the Franciscan, Minori Osservanti monks, who brought with them a revered relic, the habit that Saint Francis wore when he received the stigmata in 1224 (second chapel to the left of the high altar). The church was consecrated on August 1, 1582, and the name of Saint Saviour (San Salvatore) was added to its title. Profound changes were made: the choir was demolished and altars were added along the nave. Then, during the 17th Century, Matteo Nigetti realised the façade, widened the transept, opened windows along the nave and decorated the intervals with plasters and painted medallions. Finally, in 1770, the original truss ceiling was replaced with the current grandiose architectural framework, within which is found the *Glorification of Saint Francis* by Giuseppe Romei.

DOMENICO GHIRLANDAIO

Lamentation, Archangel Raphael, a saint (?), Mary Mother of Mercy
1472-1473
Second altar on the right, Vespucci Chapel

This is the oldest altar in the church, dating back to 1472, before the arrival of the Franciscans, according to the inscription on the tomb of Amerigo Vespucci (namesake and ancestor of the famous navigator) who was a jurist and Chancellor of the Florentine Republic under Cosimo and Piero de' Medici. The young Domenico Ghirlandaio was commissioned to decorate the chapel – the artist's first endeavour in Florence – perhaps by Amerigo himself before his death or thereafter by his heirs. The individual frescoes, painted over in 1616 and found again only in 1898, were originally linked by a series of false frames. They represent, in the lower portion at the centre, the *Lamentation*, to the left, the *Archangel Raphael* – recognisable by the remnant of a wing and Tobias whom he accompanies – to the right, a fragmentary figure, and in the lunette *Mary Mother of Mercy*. This last theme was wide-spread in Italy since the Middle Ages, though here the Virgin mercifully receives under her mantle the members of the Vespucci family together with Saint Antoninus, therefore reserving her protection to a rather narrow. The *Lamentation* also contains the portrait of a member of the Vespucci family: the character turned toward the observer. Influenced by Andrea del Castagno and Alessio Baldovinetti, his mentor, in the figure of Christ Ghirlandaio applies clear Flemish iconography.

SANDRO BOTTICELLI

Saint Augustine in his study
1480
Right wall between the third and fourth altars

DOMENICO GHIRLANDAIO

Saint Jerome in his study
1480
Left wall between the third and fourth altars

In 1480, the same year that he frescoed the refectory (p. 177), Domenico Ghirlandaio executed *Saint Jerome in his study* as the pendent, or companion piece to Botticelli's *Saint Augustine*. These frescoes, painted for the Vespucci family, were saved by Vasari when the wall partition bearing them (which once separated the choir areas from those given over to the faithful) was torn down during the work of restructuring. The compositional layouts of the two works are analogous. The two Fathers of the Church are depicted within their respective studies, surrounded by the trappings of a humanist library: the armillary sphere and Euclid's code, in Botticelli's *Saint Augustine*, folios in Hebrew and Greek, in Ghirlandaio's *Saint Jerome*. The rigorous, typically Florentine drawing and spatial design is accompanied by analytical references to Flemish art. In fact, Ghirlandaio's painting seems to be a derivation of a Van Eyck rendition of the same subject, at the time in Lorenzo il Magnifico's collection. Saint Jerome looks directly at the observer, with whom he seems almost to converse, while seeking illumination, as per the verses of the hymn in the inscription above – very wide-spread during the humanist period. Saint Augustine, instead, is caught rapt in the act of receiving divine inspiration.

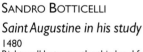

ORSANMICHELE

During the Lombard period an oratory stood here, near the Garden of San Michele. In its place Arnolfo di Cambio built a loggia where the grain market was held. This was however destroyed in a fire, and in 1337, Francesco Talenti, Neri di Fioravante and Benci di Cione built another, larger oratory. Later, when devotion grew for the miraculous image of the Madonna kept within the building, the market was transferred, the triple lancet windows closed and Orsanmichele was raised by two storeys, then used for storage. The building's role now changed. It became a true church, and in honour of the Virgin painted by Bernardo Daddi, the monumental Orcagna tabernacle was created. The Arti, the powerful guilds which permeated the city's social and economic organisation, had the honour and onus of decorating the external pillars with niches holding statues of their respective patron saints. Carried out over a period of one-hundred and fifty years, the grand project involved some of the best artists of the times: from Lorenzo Ghiberti to Donatello and Nanni di Banco, from Verrocchio to Giambologna.

DONATELLO
Tabernacle
1423

VERROCCHIO
The incredulity of Saint Thomas
1467-1483
Second tabernacle, in the centre on via Calzaiuoli

The Parte Guelfa called on Donatello to execute the centre tabernacle on the church's eastern side, in the prestigious position along the route between the Duomo and Palazzo della Signoria. Donatello must have designed it, together with the statue of *Saint Louis of Toulouse* (p. 59), in about 1423, given the evident structural analogies to Masaccio's fresco of the *Trinity* (p. 166). The sculptor executes a marble aedicule whose plinth is supported by a console enriched by two heads covered in vines, as are the proto-human masks located at the corners of the ancient sarcophagi. It was within this architecture, replete with decorative elements evoking classical art, that the Parte Guelfa set the resplendent gilded bronze statue of their patron saint. Later, they decided to transfer the statue and sell the tabernacle to the Tribunale di Mercanzia (Court of Commerce) who filled it with the statues of *Saint Thomas* and *Christ* sculpted by Verrocchio in 1483. The artist presents a bold interpretation of the celebrated encounter between resurrected Christ and the doubting apostle, setting the saint's statue just outside the niche. The two figures, enveloped in ample robes falling in wavelike folds, present a formal perfection and a harmonic composure, heightened by the precision with which the artist treated the bronze.

**ANDREA DI CIONE,
KNOW AS ORCAGNA**

Tabernacle
circa 1355-1359

BERNARDO DADDI

*Madonna and Child
with angels ("Madonna
delle Grazie")*
1347
Right aisle

After the 1348 black plague, the Company of Orsanmichele commissioned the tabernacle to the master builder and architect, Orcagna. The tabernacle was to be erected as a sign of devotion to the *Madonna delle Grazie* (Virgin of Graces), painted by Bernardo Daddi in 1347, which was then set within it. Despite its monumental dimensions, the tabernacle's complex structure is reminiscent of fine jewellery: it is inlaid with coloured marbles and stained glass. On the back, Orcagna sculpted a high relief of the *Transition* and *Assumption of the Virgin*.

SAN LORENZO

The origins of San Lorenzo coincide with the history of the Christian community in Florence. The church, dedicated to the martyred deacon, Saint Lawrence, was in fact consecrated by the bishop of Milan, Saint Ambrose, in 393. However, not a trace remains, either of that earliest Christian building or the Romanesque church constructed over it and consecrated in 1059. In 1418 Giovanni di Bicci de' Medici decided to finance transformation of the then existing church, entrusting the project to Filippo Brunelleschi, who three years later presented his design for the Basilica of San Lorenzo, located only a short distance from the Medici residence (p. 185). It was this that was to become the beloved family church of the Medici. The architect completed the Old Sacristy in 1428, though the church itself was finished by his student and biographer, Antonio Manetti in 1461. Nineteenth-century modifications to the apsidal part did not alter the integrity or harmony of Brunelleschi's interior, based on precise proportional relationships and separated into nave and two side aisles by columns with Corinthian capitals and round arches, above which courses a jutting cornice. The classical architectural framework in *pietra serena* stands out against the white plaster facing. The façade's architect was to be Michelangelo, appointed to the task by Pope Leo X. However, the project was never realised, though the artist did complete the Tribuna or balcony on the interior wall of the façade, from which the Holy Relics were displayed to the faithful.

ROSSO FIORENTINO

Marriage of the Virgin

1523
Right aisle, second chapel (Ginori Chapel)

Incongruously, it is the consummate Medici church, San Lorenzo, where this celebrated painting is found. Incongruous, because its author, Rosso Fiorentino, never performed a single work for powerful family, who more and more came to dominate Florence. This work, in fact, was commissioned by Carlo Ginori. The painter adds a great deal of anecdotes extraneous to the event of the *Marriage of the Virgin*, set in a dark narrow interior crowded with characters superimposed one on the other, amongst which Saint Apollonias can be discerned crouched in the foreground and, behind her, the Dominican saint, Vincenzo Ferrer. Saint Joseph is represented as a handsome youth, in stark contrast with the apocryphal Gospel that describes him as an elderly carpenter. Such liberties, and the artist's recourse to early 15th-century models underscore Rosso's highly independent figurative style, never entirely accepted in Florence.

DESIDERIO DA SETTIGNANO
Tabernacle
circa 1461
Right aisle, between the last chapel and transept

The marble tabernacle, a refined work by Desiderio da Settignano fully restored in 1956, is located in the basilica's right aisle. Sculpted around 1461, the ciborium is gracefully composed of a delicate bas-relief portraying the *Pietà*. Above, set between two candle holders in the form of angels, is the niche where the Sacrament was held. The niche was created with judicious perspective effects imparted by the lacunar vault and sideways foreshortening of the arches, from which two adoring angels look out. Overall, the architecture is monumental in style, with rich embossed decoration on the elements that go to make up its cornice. On the fastigium, according to a wide-spread tradition, *Child Jesus in the act of blessing*, is set between two small angels and cherub heads in the lunette. The delicate elegance and precision of the sculptural surface serves to underscore the importance and devotion invested to stone tabernacles of this type during the Renaissance. They were in fact very wide spread during the 15th and 16th Centuries.

DONATELLO AND COLLABORATORS
Pulpits with Stories of the Passion and Resurrection of Christ
1461-1465
Last span

These pulpits are the utmost expression of the art of Donatello, who died without ever having completed them. The place the works were originally intended for is unknown. They were used for the first time in 1515, mounted provisionally on two wood frameworks for the arrival of Pope Leo X in Florence, and subsequently installed on the current supporting marble columns between 1558 and 1565. Although the contribution of the elderly sculptor's assistants is evident in the reliefs, the expressive power originating in Donatello's religious fervour remains nevertheless intact, especially in his representation of the episodes of the *Passion of Christ*, to the left, and the *Resurrection*, to the right. In these, the last years of the artist's life, he abandoned traditional iconography and gave vent to the turmoil of his soul as he felt death draw near, depicting all the energy and intensity of the expressions on the faces of the scene's participants.

Donatello, *Pulpit of the Passion*   Donatello, *Pulpit of the Resurrection*

147

Old Sacristy

The Old Sacristy, the true royal chapel of the Medici, was built by will of Giovanni di Bicci de' Medici and dedicated to Saint John the Evangelist. Brunelleschi completed the structure itself in 1429, and Donatello saw to its decoration. It therefore represents the synthesis of High Renaissance Art. It is a cubic dome-topped structure with ribbing in pietra serena, which was also used for the other structural members, so as to clearly highlight the framework against the plaster walls, thus forming the background from which the exquisite painted plasters by Donatello stand out: the tondi in the pendentives with Scenes from the life of Saint John the Evangelist and the four Evangelists; the frieze with cherubs and seraphs; Saints Cosmas and Damian, Stephen and Lawrence in the large lunettes above the bronze doors (also by Donatello), representing Martyrs, the Apostles and the Church Fathers presented two by two in agitated poses. At the centre, under the marble shelf with porphyry disks, a material evocative of antiquity and a symbol of sovereignty and stability, is Buggiano's sarcophagus of Giovanni di Bicci and his wife Piccarda Bueri, the parents of Cosimo il Vecchio. Buggiano, Brunelleschi's adopted son, was also the author of the altar in the apse, where the frescoed dome represents the Zodiac as seen from Florence on the night of July 4, 1442.

VERROCCHIO

Sarcophagus of Piero and Giovanni de' Medici
1472
Old Sacristy

For the sepulchre of their father, Piero il Gottoso, and uncle, Giovanni, Lorenzo il Magnifico and his brother Giuliano turned to Verrocchio, erudite and refined artist, as well as goldsmith, painter and sculptor. Verrocchio's skill in, and devotion to all these arts are manifest together in this renaissance masterpiece. The work, in fact, was to have a great influence on Verrochio's young pupil, Leonardo da Vinci (p. 24). It is with the master painter's eye that Verrocchio balances the urn's red porphyry with the medallion's green serpentine, two materials evoking the deeds of imperial antiquity, and the white marble of the floral frieze with the bronze of the fretwork and decorations. The sarcophagus is conceived of as a jewel case within an elaborate setting: luxuriant leaves of hyacinth overlying the mighty lion-paw legs, opulent cornucopias amongst which is the family coat of arms, the garland surrounding the inscription that continues in the marble base upheld by the naturalistic turtles, and, finally, the extraordinary woven cord.

FILIPPO LIPPI

Annunciation
1437-1441
Left transept, to the left,
Martelli Chapel

This altarpiece was painted by Filippo Lippi between 1437 and 1441 for the altar of the chapel where Niccolò Martelli, a sponsor of the church's reconstruction, was buried. The scene in the left foreground is rich with fanciful elements, such as the two angels, which although departing from traditional iconography, serve to animate the narrative scheme. Symbolic elements also abound, such as the ampoule on the steps alluding to Mary's virginity. Such details, from simple scenic elements are transformed into the components of a still-life of the highest calibre. Perspective is played upon on different planes, defining great depth into which one's gaze is lost in the far-reaching space from the portico to the looming towers of the city in the background. The work is completed by a predella with *Stories of Saint Nicholas* by the hand of Giovanni di Francesco, a collaborator of Filippo Lippi.

BRONZINO

Martyrdom of Saint Lawrence
1565-1569
Left aisle, last span

This large fresco was unveiled to the public on August 10, 1569, the day in which the city celebrated Saint Lawrence, the church's patron saint. Bronzino portrayed himself to the left under the statue of Mercury, the guardian of artists, next to his maestro, Pontormo (who had died twelve years prior) and accompanied by another youth, perhaps his favoured student, Alessandro Allori. Against a classical architectural background, the composition, crowded with figures in affected poses, forced foreshortening and Mannerist torsion, is a homage to Michelangelo. Although it was not his last work, Bronzino, by now elderly, wished to leave this fresco as his artistic testament. In fact, he died a few years after its completion, on November 23,1572.

Medici-Laurentian Library

It was pope Clement VII who, in 1523, entrusted Michelangelo with construction of the library which was to house the rich collection of miniated codices begun by Cosimo il Vecchio. Michelangelo designed the architecture and followed its construction up to his transfer to Rome in 1534, when Vasari and Ammannati, faithfully adhering to Michelangelo's plan, brought it to completion in 1568. The entrance to the library is through a corridor set between the church and the first cloister, leading to the wonderful vestibule, an architectural delight whose wonders are revealed in its towering heights: twin columns on consoles set deeply into the wall to mask their load-bearing function and false windows opening onto aedicules. The same energy that Michelangelo unleashed as a sculptor animates the walls of this singular room. The staircase executed by Ammannati leads to the reading room, whose architectural plan is developed instead along its length. It is an environment of great formal homogeneity: the carved wooden ceiling, the floor in terracotta and the monumental benches with stands holding some of the most important manuscripts in the world, still in their original positions.

Michelangelo Buonarroti, *Vestibule*
Michelangelo Buonarroti, *Reading Room*

SAN MINIATO AL MONTE

Masterpiece of Florentine romanesque architecture, the basilica of San Miniato al Monte built by will of Bishop Ildebrando in 1018 on the site where he claimed to have found the mortal remains of the martyred saint, Miniato. The task of its building continued for centuries and was completed only in 1207, the date inscribed on the church's pavement. Its structure, in fact, reflects the various stages of its construction, even its geometrically patterned marble façade. The lower part, done in the 11th Century, follows a more rigorous, logical layout, unfolding in five arcades with two glass panels alternating with three portals, while the upper, least coherent section, added from the 12th Century, has at its centre a gabled window surmounted by a thirteenth-century mosaic and a pediment decorated by symbolic motifs overhung by an eagle clawing at the bale of cloth. The same green and white colours of the façade are repeated in its interior. The space is divided into three aisles by pillars of various styles, alternating with twin columns topped by Corinthian or Romanesque water-leal capitals. The intarsia marble pavement extends like a carpet before one's feet and in its fourth section bears a *Zodiac* replete with symbolic allusions.

MICHELOZZO, LUCA DELLA ROBBIA AND MASO DI BARTOLOMEO

Chapel of the Crucifix
1447-1452
Central aisle, to the centre

The Calimala Guild, who oversaw the church's maintenance since the 13th Century, requested that a tabernacle be built in the centre of the nave to serve as worthy setting for the revered crucifix of Saint John Gualberto (moved to the church of Santa Trinita in 1671). Piero de' Medici therefore commissioned Michelozzo with its creation. The architect was helped in the undertaking by Maso di Bartolomeo, author of the bronze eagles, and Luca della Robbia, who covered the exterior of the barrel vault with enamelled terracotta in the Medici colours (red, white and green) and its inside with gold-highlighted lacunars. The Medici emblem is recurrent in the frieze, the lateral volutes of the crowning and in the medallion on the back of the aedicule, a light and elegant structure holding the panels painted by Agnolo Gaddi between 1394 and 1396.

FLORENTINE MASTERS
Pulpit
Late 12th - early 13th Century
Presbytery

The pulpit, supported by two columns with composite capitals, it is grafted onto the iconostasis decorated with inlaid marble plutei with oriental geometric motifs. A veritable jewel of Romanesque art, its square case is adorned by extremely vivid figures. The lectern is supported by an eagle set on a telamon, which is, in turn, upheld by a lion.

MOSAICIST OF THE LATE 13th CENTURY
Enthroned Christ between the Virgin and Saint Minias with symbols of the Evangelists
1297
Apse

Christ Pantocrator – the "be all and end all", as symbolised by the Greek letters A and Ω is enthroned between the Virgin and Saint Minias. The saint, martyred in 250 during the persecution of Christians by the Emperor Decius, sets down his crown in a gesture of humility. The accompanying inscription proclaims him king of Armenia. The glistening mosaic decoration is completed by the symbols of the four Evangelists and, on the left, the small kneeing figure bearing a gift. This refined mosaic adopts a cultured pictorial language, rich in symbolic references. Originally executed in 1297, it was restored twice, once by the painter Alessio Baldovinetti in the late 15th and once in the 19th Century.

Chapel of the Cardinal of Portugal
Left aisle

This sacellum, the most richly decorated of the 15th Century Florentine votive chapels, is set under a lacunared arch, bearing an inscription referring to the chapel's construction. It was completed in 1466 to house the mortal remains of the young cardinal of Portugal, Jacopo di Lusitania, who died in Florence in August, 1459. It is the fruit of a particularly felicitous collaboration amongst a number of fine artists and craftsman. The architecture is by Antonio Manetti, who died before its completion; the polychrome enamelled vault with illusory motifs was decorated by Luca della Robbia in graded-blue medallions, depicting the Cardinal Virtues and the Holy Spirit; Antonio Rossellino sculpted the sumptuous sepulchre and other marble furnishings; Antonio and Piero del Pollaiolo painted the altarpiece, replaced by a copy, the original is in the Uffizi (p. 19); Alessio Baldovinetti did the frescoes; and finally, specialised masters realised the square hall's pavement. A perfect equilibrium is attained between the architecture's geometry, profiled by its *pietra serena* members, and the exultation of the colours.

SANTA CROCE

The Basilica of Santa Croce, designed by Arnolfo di Cambio, was built to replace the smaller church which once stood on the same site. The first stone was laid on May 3, 1294 and the construction progressed so quickly that by the architect's death in 1302, the apse section and adjacent chapels had already been finished. The original project was completed in about 1385. Its interior, in the form of an Egyptian cross with wooden roof trusses (as in all Franciscan churches) and terracotta floor, is sober and ample, solemnly partitioned by stout pillars sustaining ogival arches, above of which courses the gallery. The interior's illumination comes from tall narrow stained-glass windows, the oldest of which, dating back to the 14th Century, are found at the transept. It was here that the most prestigious and affluent Florentine families competed for the honour of having a chapel – to the glory of God and, above all, their own names – turning to Giotto or his most faithful student, Taddeo Gaddi, or to Bernardo Daddi or Maso di Banco for its decoration. In the late 14th Century the work of adorning the church was continued by Giovanni da Milano, Agnolo Gaddi and the epigones of the Tuscan school of Giotto, Niccolò di Pietro Gerini and Spinello Aretino. Thus, the history of 14th-century painting is represented in its entirety at Santa Croce. In 1442 the basilica was finally consecrated by Pope Eugenius IV, and three years later Bernardo Rossellino created the funeral monument to Leonardo Bruni, the first in a long series of illustrious tombs. Michelangelo and the statesman, Machiavelli, the scientist, Galileo Galilei, the playwright, Vittorio Alfieri and the poet, Ugo Foscolo, who had celebrated the "urns of the mighty" in his *Dei Sepolcri*, and lastly, the musician, Gioacchino Rossini, were all laid to rest here; even Dante, who died in exile in Ravenna where he is buried, had a cenotaph here. Thus, Santa Croce, completed in the mid 19th Century with the addition of the façade and bell tower, became the Pantheon of civil and artistic glories.

**GIORGIO VASARI,
BATTISTA LORENZI,
VALERIO CIOLI,
GIOVANNI BANDINI,
GIOVAN BATTISTA
NALDINI**

Tomb of Michelangelo
1564-1578
Right aisle, after the first altar

Commissioned by his nephew Leonardo, this funeral monument was placed here on the site of the Buonarroti family graves at the express wish of Michelangelo himself. Giorgio Vasari designed it in 1564, though the monument itself was not begun for another four years, being delayed by the completion of the tomb's masonry work and the arrival of the marbles – the white 'Carrara' and grained 'Serravezza' varieties for the sarcophagus. A dispute then broke out between Vasari and Michelangelo's nephew over the Supremacy of the Arts, and therefore over which art form, *Sculpture* or *Painting* was to have the place of honour at the sarcophagus' centre. This caused considerable delays and forced Battista Lorenzi, a pupil of Baccio Bandinelli, to transform the allegorical figure of *Sculpture* he had originally been assigned into *Painting*. The resulting *Painting* is now found at the left, and, in fact, in confirmation of the conversion performed, is holding a model in its hand, the specific attribute of *Sculpture*. Also, the brushes and palette have been relegated to under the base. In the centre is *Sculpture*, by Valerio Cioli, and to the right *Architecture*, by Giovanni Bandini, known as Opera because he had worked for twenty years on the cathedral (l'Opera del Duomo) side by side with his maestro, Bandinelli. *Architecture* and *Sculpture* present the traditional iconography: the former with compass, design scroll and a capital, the latter with chisel in hand. Michelangelo's bust is also by Lorenzi. Finally, Giovan Battista Naldini, a pupil of Vasari, is the author of the fresco of the *Deposition* and the painted architecture with the great canopy upheld by winged puti, perhaps an addition made at a later time. The emblem of the three interlacing crowns was not chosen by Michelangelo, but is the fruit of a later conception. Michelangelo is buried in front of the second altar, where the tombstone was placed flanked by the Buonarroti family's coat of arms.

Antonio Canova
Tomb of Vittorio Alfieri
1810
Right aisle, after the third altar

Vittorio Alfieri and the German princess, Louise van Stolberg, at the time married to the Count of Albany, met on the shores of the Arno River. After the death of her husband, the couple settled in Florence, where they lived together from 1793 until Alfieri's death in 1803. The Countess of Albany had ancient graves removed in order to be able to erect the funeral monument to her poet in 1810. Antonio Canova, the neo-classic sculptor much in demand throughout Europe, received the commission and executed it, in his own words, "in a sober and stately style, in order for the character of the work to match the boldness of the pen" of the acclaimed poet. Alfieri is portrayed in the medallion, mourned by towered Italy, the very first representation of this iconographic motif in sculpture. The lira and masks allude to the tragedies which earned Alfieri his renown.

Benedetto da Maiano

Pulpit with Stories of Saint Francis
1481-1487
Third pillar to the right

In 1487, the pulpit was already standing at the third pillar, that is, in the middle of the area given over to worship. Keeping in mind that at the time the church was divided by a partition wall demolished in the following century, it was therefore set in a position where the five reliefs with Stories of Saint Francis were clearly visible. There is the scene of the Marrakech martyrdom of the early martyrs, canonised by the Franciscan pope, Sesto IV in 1481, which is rather rare in cycles devoted to the saint. However, apart from constituting a useful reference point for dating the pulpit, it also furnishes a key to its reading, linked to precise historical events: these were the years when the Turkish threat was becoming ever more pressing, and the papacy, together with the Franciscan order, was calling for a new crusade. The pulpit was donated by the rich merchant, Pietro Mellini, whose wrinkled, keen countenance was immortalised by Benedetto da Maiano in the 1474 bust now at the Bargello. When the pulpit was being placed, the monks feared that church's structures would collapse, as the plan called for perforating the pillar itself to insert the steps providing access to the pulpit. In the end, this clever solution was adopted, in which it is supposed, the architect Giuliano da Maiano, brother of Benedetto, had had a hand. In this way, viewing the pulpit from the central aisle, it seems suspended, resting on the corbel and console, amongst niches faced in red marble bearing the Virtues. At the pillar's base is Mellini's marble-panelled tombstone, which duplicates the pulpit's layout.

DONATELLO
Annunciation
circa 1435
Right aisle, after the fifth altar

This dazzling tabernacle, made from hard sandstone embellished by gilding, was the altarpiece of the Cavalcanti family, whose coats of arms are set in the plinth. As in a sacred representation, the Angel and Virgin, in natural dimensions and nearly full relief, occupy the space between two pilasters before a panelled background, where, apart from a front view of the throne, nothing indulges in narrative, even the traditional lily-filled vase is lacking. Everything is focused on the mute eloquence of the gestures: the kneeing Angel in the act of worshipful blessing and the surprised Virgin, withdrawing almost out of the scene. The firm figures of their bodies is hinted at under the rich flowing robes. The solemn tone of the *Annunciation* is counterbalanced by the playfulness of the puti perched restlessly on the pediment whorls. The overlying aedicule is decorated in classical motifs, probably inspired to Donatello by his Roman visit, whence he had just returned in 1433.

BERNARDO ROSSELLINO
Tomb of Leonardo Bruni
1445-1447
Right aisle, after a side door following the fifth altar

The sepulchral monument to Leonardo Bruni, chancellor of the Florentine Republic, attributed by historical sources to Bernardo Rossellino, set a new standard for such sepulchres. In this work, in fact, Rossellino seeks the ideal union between architecture and sculpture, an endeavour stemming from his affinity for the humanistic tradition, which in art translated into a rigorous architectural scheme, such as that typical of Leon Battista Alberti's work, a collaborator of the sculptor. A great arch sustained by pilasters frames the niche enclosing the sarcophagus and coffin on which Leonardo Bruni rests. Bruni, whose somatic qualities are depicted with great precision, holds in his crossed hands a copy of his *History of Florence*. The monument's dominant element is the commemoration of the deceased and his culture, humanistically intended as an example for future generations to follow. The only religious reference is the tondo in the lunette, portraying the *Madonna and Child between two orant angels*. This work is considered the prototype of fifteenth-century tombs, from which numerous others have descended, such as the monument to Carlo Marsuppini by Desiderio da Settignano in the opposite aisle of the church.

Giotto

Stories of Saint John the Baptist and Saint John the Evangelist
circa 1310-1313
Transept, second chapel to the right of the main chapel, Peruzzi Chapel

According to historical sources, Giotto painted four chapels in the Franciscan church. Today, only two remain: this, the Peruzzi Chapel, and the adjacent one for the Bardi family, both rich and powerful Florentine banker families. The history of these two chapels is, in fact, identical: the decoration was plastered over in the mid-18th Century, to be rediscovered only the following century. They have since both been subjected to heavy restorative operations. Moreover, the wall frescoes of the Peruzzi Chapel with the *Stories of Saint John the Baptist*, to the left, and *Saint John the Evangelist*, to the right, were performed almost entirely on already dried surfaces, a rapid technique that was perhaps employed by Giotto and his workshop because of their many commitments. Despite the poor state of conservation, we can nonetheless appreciate the varied and complex relationships between the figures and space, especially in the episodes whose architecture runs obliquely, as the chapel's room is high and narrow. After his frescoes in Assisi and Padua, here Giotto sought a highly monumental tone.

Ascension of Saint John the Evangelist

Funeral Rites of Saint Francis

GIOTTO
Stories of Saint Francis
circa 1325
transept, first chapel to the right
of the main chapel,
Bardi Chapel

Giotto, on commission to the Bardi family, illustrated some of the central events in the life of Saint Francis. This work was destined to become a paradigm for Florentine painters of the 14th Century, beginning with his faithful pupil, Taddeo Gaddi, who in the cabinets of the sacristy of Santa Croce (now in the Gallery of the Accademia, p. 42) would make clear reference to it. The buildings in the lunettes are ingeniously foreshortened, as Giotto took into careful account the point in the chapel's centre from which the fresco would be viewed. As in the adjoining Peruzzi Chapel, there is sense of space that animates this, the last stage in the painter's career. The solemn gestures of the friars, so charged with humanity, in the *Funeral Rites of Saint Francis*, represent one of the unforgettable pages in Italian Art. On the chapel altar, the panel portraying *Saint Francis and twenty scenes from his life* is by an anonymous painter, one of the most significant figures in the early 13th-century Florence.

DONATELLO
Crucifix
circa 1412
Left transept, Bardi di Vernio Chapel

The crucifix was probably sculpted by Donatello in around 1412, although some scholars set it in the third decade of the 15th Century. The sculpture seems to document the transition between two artistic epochs, from gothic sculpture to plastic naturalism, the hallmark of renaissance art, with which the Donatello's early works were permeated. In fact, Christ's figure on the cross is represented with true realism: the contrast between the tortured elegance of his body and the intensity of his face has long prompted dissonant judgements. In fact, according to a famous anecdote, recounted by Vasari in his *Lives of the Most Eminent Painters, Sculptors and Architects*, Brunelleschi reproached Donatello for having set a peasant's figure on the cross instead of the delicate and perfect body of Christ. The crucifix's arms are attached to the body by means of pivots that allow arranging them in either of two positions: "in cross" or "in pietà". During its restoration two additional iron plates were discovered to have been inserted at the wrists, as if the artist had decided that the arms were perhaps to short, and lengthened them accordingly. No one can ever say whether this was the fruit of long deliberation or prompted by criticism such as that attributed to Brunelleschi.

SANTA FELICITA

Despite its current 18th-century appearance, the origins of this church, dedicated to the Roman martyr, Saint Felicity, date back, like San Lorenzo, to the 4th Century, when an early Christian basilica was founded by the flourishing Syrian-Greek community, of which extensive epigraphic evidence has been found. In the 11th Century a Romanesque church was raised on the site of the old church, and remained intact up to the 18th Century, though with a number of additions: the 14th-century Chapter House, with frescoes by Niccolò di Pietro Gerini (1387), the Barbadori Chapel built by Brunelleschi in 1420, which was later taken over by the Capponi family and decorated by Pontormo, and the sacristy in the style of Brunelleschi. In 1565, by will of Cosimo I, Vasari built the corridor that linked Palazzo Vecchio to Pitti Palace, and the church took on new importance, as it could be reached through the corridor passing above the façade's portico, thus allowing the grand duke's family to participate in religious functions from the inside loggia. From 1736 to 1739 Ferdinando Ruggieri remodelled the interior, aspiring to renaissance models and sparing the Barbadori-Capponi chapel, as well as that of the Canigiani family on the opposite side and the seventeenth-century choir designed by Cigoli. On the third altar on the right, the 1863 altarpiece by Antonio Ciseri represents *Saint Felicity and the martyrdom of the Maccabei brothers*.

Deposition, detail, *Nicodemus*

PONTORMO AND BRONZINO

Deposition, Annunciation and the Evangelists
1525-1528
Nave, to the right, Capponi Chapel

The chapel devoted to Maria Annunciata was chosen by the rich banker Ludovico Capponi as the burial place for his own family. Pontormo worked here in total isolation between 1525 and 1528. According to an iconographic design probably suggested by Capponi, the pictorial decoration centres round the theme of the Resurrection of the soul, as revealed by Jesus Christ's death. Beginning with the *Annunciation*, painted on the entrance wall of the church, Pontormo transcends traditional iconography and depicts the Virgin turned toward the great altarpiece portraying the *Deposition*, and the angel, in the moments immediately following the annunciation, in ecstatic contemplation of the divine light. The entire path to redemption seems clear: from worldly life to the hopes of a return to paradise after death. In fact, it is not physical or psychological pain which Pontormo depicts on the faces of the characters surrounding Christ, he, himself self-absorbed in serene peace, but on the contrary, the dumb-stricken awe of those faced with the fulfilment of the divine plan. In the bodies that seem to challenge the force of gravity and the changing interplay of clear colours, the painting seems to strive more evocation than representation, an evident emulation of Michelangelo's art. The iconography is completed by the tondi with the four *Evangelists* in the pendentive, one of whom, *Saint Mark* (the bearded youth) is by Portormo's pupil, Agnolo Bronzino. A fresco once on the dome representing *God the Father* bordered by the four patriarchs has unfortunately been lost.

SANTA MARIA DEL CARMINE

The first foundation stone of this church in honour of the Blessed Virgin of Mount Carmel was set in 1268 and, although the building was consecrated in 1436, its construction continued throughout the entire 15th Century, to be completed only in 1476. However, little of that earliest structure survives. What we see today is due in part to the modifications ordered by grand duke Cosimo I in 1568 to comply with the norms set

Below:
Masaccio, *Tribute Money*
Below to left:
Filippino Lippi, *Imprisoned Saint Peter visited by Saint Paul*

forth by the Ecumenical council (at the time, Vasari was in fact busy on similar alterations to other Florentine churches). However, the greatest changes to the church were the consequence of the dreadful fire that in 1771 destroyed most of the building, miraculously sparing the two chapels at the ends of the transept, the Brancacci and Corsini Chapels. Reconstruction was entrusted to the architect Giuseppe Ruggieri and continued by his pupil. It was concluded in 1775, shortly after which Giuseppe Romei and Domenico Stagi frescoed the dome and the vaults of the nave, transept and choir.

160

Below:
Masaccio and Filippino
Lippi, *Saint Peter bringing
Theophilus' son to life* and
Peter enthroned

Below at right:
Masaccio, *Saint Peter healing
with his shadow*

MASACCIO, MASOLINO, FILIPPINO LIPPI

Stories of Saint Peter
circa 1424-1427 and 1485
Right transept, Brancacci Chapel

Commissioned in 1424 by Felice Brancacci from Masolino and Masaccio, the chapel's decoration represents one of the most extraordinary fresco series of the Renaissance and would constitute a paragon for future generations of painters. The two artists worked together at first. Then, after Masolino was called to Hungary, the work was continued by Masaccio alone until 1427, and finally completed in the mid-1580s by Filippino Lippi. The frescoes provide a good opportunity to compare the serene, yet gothic elegance of Masolino's painting with the expressive power of Masaccio, who opens up new directions in the use of light, the representation of plastic attributes and the rendering of perspective. The scenes are powerful drama: the *Expulsion from Paradise*, with Adam and Eve pursued by their own remorse, the grandiose scene of the *Tribute Money*, and the expressiveness of Saint Peter's gesture towards the splendid kneeing nude in *Saint Peter Baptising*. Masaccio appears to have distanced himself far from the elegant grace of Masolino's representations, such as the *Original Sin* or *Saint Peter healing a lame man and bringing Tabitha to life*, although in the animated scenes of everyday life in the background the painter seems perhaps to experiment with the new idiom adopted by his pupil. Despite their differences, through their *Stories of Saint Peter* both artists however express their affirmation of the Church as the fundamental means for man's salvation, while in Florence, man, through his psychological and moral centrality, was being viewed as

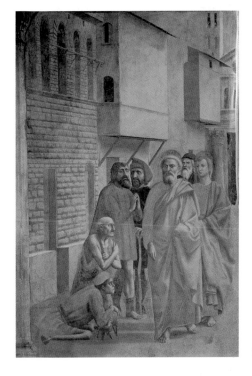

Masolino, *Saint Peter healing the lame man and bringing Tabitha to life*

the absolute moving force. When Felice Brancacci fell into disgrace, the monks changed the chapel's title, dedicating it to the Madonna of the People, and placed on its altar the revered altarpiece portraying *Enthroned Madonna and Child with angels*, known as the "*Madonna del Popolo*", work of the so-called Maestro di Sant'Agata and dated to about 1268.

Corsini Chapel
Left transept

A famous example of late Florentine baroque, this opulent chapel miraculously escaped the 1771 fire, except for its façade, which was redone in the original design. It was first set up in 1675 at the request of the marquises Bartolomeo and Neri Corsini to honour their Carmelite ancestor, Andrea, canonised in 1629. The architect Pier Francesco Silvani demolished the former gothic chapel and arranged the new one in the form of a Greek cross, entirely faced in marble, and set a façade at its entrance, on whose tympanum are two plaster angels upholding the coat of arms of the Corsini family, to this day still patrons of the chapel. On the opposite wall, the precious urn holding the remains of the saint is richly decorated by a silver embossed relief where Giovan Battista Foggini depicted the funeral, veneration and canonisation of Saint Andrea. Above is the marble altarpiece with the glorified saint, a collaborative work by Foggini and Balthasar Permoser. The Florentine sculptor also did the splendid reliefs overlying the tombs on the side walls, depicting the *Apparition of the Madonna*, to the left, and *Saint Andrea guiding the Florentines in the Battle of Anghiari*, to the right. In this latter, the heroic animated scene seems barely contained within the bounds of the frame. In 1682 the chapel was topped with a luminous dome by Luca Giordano, bearing the swirling apotheosis of the saint, while the pendentive depicts his virtues.

SANTA MARIA NOVELLA

The construction of Santa Maria Novella over the structures of a pre-existing church was begun in 1278 by the Dominican monks Fra Sisto and Fra Ristoro. The work continued for nearly a century and was almost complete by the mid 14th Century, when the façade was begun. The lower portion of the façade is, in fact, gothic with its acute avelli (tomb vaults) and two small portals, while the interior is done in Cistercian architecture, divided into three ample aisles by pillars of various styles bearing round and ogival arches and cross vaults. Amongst the first works of art to arrive here was the *Maestà*, now in the Uffizi (p. 12), which the Company of the Laudesi commissioned from Duccio di Buoninsegna in 1285. The *Crucifix* by Giotto is documented to shortly thereafter, as early as 1312. It was however after the 1348 plague that the greatest decorative undertakings were begun in the Strozzi Chapel by Nardo di Cione and his brother Andrea, and in the Chapter House where Andrea di Bonaiuto frescoed the manifesto of the Dominican order (p. 86). The great artists of the Renaissance, Masaccio and Brunelleschi, Ghiberti and Paolo Uccello, have all left their marks in Santa Maria Novella. The façade was completed in the 15th Century, in 1470 according to the inscription, next to which is the name of the enterprise's patron, the wealthy businessman, Giovanni Rucellai. Rucellai commissioned the work from Leon Battista Alberti, the architect who had designed his residence (p. 187). Alberti added the main en-

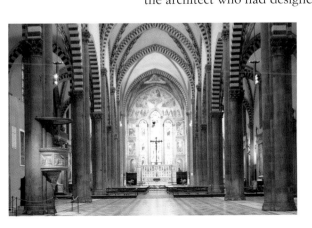

tranceway and continued the façade beginning with the frieze bearing the Rucellai emblem (a full sail in the wind). He adopted the technique of black and white marbles to create wholly Renaissance geometric designs in harmonious proportional relationships. Ghirlandaio, and even perhaps young Michelangelo, Benedetto da Maiano and Filippino Lippi were called on by the Tornabuoni and Filippo Strozzi, nearly in competition. And finally, Santa Maria Novella underwent extensive modifications, ordered by Cosimo I and carried out by Vasari, according to the dictates of the Counter Reformation.

DOMENICO GHIRLANDAIO AND WORKSHOP

Stories of the Virgin
1485-1490
Main chapel,
Tornabuoni Chapel

The decoration of the church's Main Chapel was commissioned from Domenico Ghirlandaio and his flourishing workshop by the wealthy and powerful Tornabuoni family, entrepreneurs and bankers allied with the Medici. Very much in demand at the end of the 15ᵗʰ Century, Ghirlandaio headed, together with his brothers Davide and Benedetto, a very well organised family enterprise with many skilled pupils and collaborators, including at the time of the chapel frescoes, young Michelangelo. The cycle depicts *Scenes from the life of Mary* and *John the Baptist*, in which the author's happy narrative vein is exalted, especially in the intimate family scenes. The characters are set in richly decorated, courtly surroundings, as in the touching *Birth of the Virgin*, or within typical Florentine homes, as in the *Birth of John the Baptist*. The choral scenes clearly reveal the workshop's contribution: the settings possess a certain coldness, though the beautiful portrait groups, a speciality in which Ghirlandaio excelled, are charmingly rendered. Some claim to discern the hand of young Michelangelo in some of the figures in the series, for instance the nudes that on occasion appear to the scenes' sides. In any event, this is an exemplary work that was to become a model for the up and coming generation of painters, such as Raphael and Fra Bartolomeo.

Domenico Ghirlandaio, *Zacharias writes down his son's name*,
detail of *Stories of John the Baptist*

FILIPPO LIPPI

Stories of Saints Phillip and John the Evangelist
1487-1502

BENEDETTO DA MAIANO

Tomb of Filippo Strozzi
1490-1495
Right transept, first chapel to the right of the main chapel,
Chapel of Filippo Strozzi

The Strozzi family had always considered the church to be a sort of personal sepulchre when in 1486 Filippo Strozzi acquired the Chapel of Saint John the Evangelist, to the right of the choir. On the one hand, he wished to celebrate the family to which he had devoted his life, while on the other, he felt compelled to outdo the Tornabuoni, who had recently charged Ghirlandaio with an important fresco series in the same church. For the pictorial decoration, the Strozzi chose Filippino Lippi, an artist following the new trends set by da Vinci, and whose style had little in common with Ghirlandaio's serene elegance. Indeed, perhaps due to its drawn-out execution – from 1487 to 1502 – the chapel is clearly the work of a mature artist, by now far removed from the certainties of the 15ᵗʰ Century. It is pervaded by a vibrant restlessness that translates into a vital, active representation crowded with characters in a setting of grandiose scenes and imposing architecture derived from ancient, though fancifully revisited, models. The precious sepulchre by Benedetto da Maiano is found in an almost concealed position on the back wall– testimony to the rejection of Humanist glorification of personal achievements. The artist uses iconography that, beginning with the theme of death, ascends through the sophisticated play of illusory elements, for the most part in black and white, up to the glass door with *Saints Phillip, John and the Virgin*, to culminate in the triumph of *Fame* and *Eternity*. The left wall bears frescoes of scenes from the life of *Saint John the Evangelist*, while the right wall is devoted to the life of *Saint Phillip*.

FILIPPO BRUNELLESCHI

Crucifix
circa 1425-1430
Left transept, first chapel to the left of the main chapel,
Gondi Chapel

The back wall of the Gondi Chapel, designed by Giuliano da Sangallo in the early 16th Century, holds the *Crucifix* which, according to the anecdote recounted by Vasari, Brunelleschi sculpted in response to Donatello's (p. 157). Brunelleschi's intent was to show how anatomy was to be depicted, in contrast to the dramatic expressiveness of Donatello's Christ. The work, in fact, seeks to render divine perfection through formal perfection according to precise rules of proportion: the span of Christ's open arms corresponds exactly to the *Crucifix*'s height. No pain seems to disturb Christ's body, whose anatomy – stemming from careful study of classical sculptures – reveals the muscles and tendons beneath the skin of the Thorax. It is an intellectual meditation that takes on universal significance.

NARDO DI CIONE

Paradise, Last Judgement, Hell and the Purgatory
circa 1350-1357

ANDREA DI CIONE (KNOW AS ORCAGNA)

Christ Risen giving the keys to Saint Peter and a book to Saint Thomas, Madonna, Saint John the Baptist and other saints
1357
Left transept, Strozzi Chapel

In 1350 Tommaso di Rossello Strozzi, in the hopes of expiating his sins of usury, donated the decoration of the church chapel built in the left transept around 1335. The frescoes were entrusted to Nardo di Cione, who executed the *Last Judgement* on the back wall, designed its splendid stained-glass window, and painted *Heaven*, *Purgatory* and *Hell* on the side walls. The iconographic design followed by the artist was very much in fashion at the time, an epoch in which the memories of the plague that had flagellated Europe was still very much alive. The frescoes' uniform style exalts Cioni's more pictorial skill, careful in the physiognomic rendition and psychological study of the characters. In contrast, his more celebrated brother, Andrea, called Orcagna, was both sculptor and painter, and the author of the coeval panel on the altar, signed and dated 1357, representing *Christ Risen giving the keys to Saint Peter and a book to Saint Thomas, Madonna, Saint John the Baptist and other saints*. The structural composition of the altarpiece is rather peculiar in that the typical polyptych division adopted is only illusory: the partitions are simply painted on.

GIOTTO
Crucifix
circa 1290
Sacristy

The *Crucifix* of Saint Maria Novella represents a radical departure from the preceding Byzantine-like tradition of the 13th Century, which called for the physiognomy of Christ's body to be rendered in rigorously stylised fashion. In this *Crucifix*, already mentioned in a document from 1312, Giotto surpasses such iconography and inaugurates a style that was to attain much success. Christ hangs from the cross borne down with the full weight of his body, his feet are pierced by a single nail, the hands cupped and the hair dangling on the tilted side of his head. The robes of *Sorrowful Mary* and *Saint John* are flecked with the gilded highlighting typical of the thirteenth-century idiom, the inheritance of Cimabue, his maestro. By such figurative conventions alone the panel can be dated to the last decade of the 13th Century, that is, immediately after Giotto frescoed the main Basilica in Assisi.

MASACCIO
Trinity
circa 1427
Left aisle, third span

The *Trinity* seems to have been wholly invested with the rigorous principles of Brunelleschi. Following the prescripts studied and set forth by his architect friend, Masaccio sets down a scene in carefully constructed perspective. In fact, a direct contribution by Brunelleschi has even been postulated. In this fresco, completed shortly few before his departure for Rome, the artist seeks to prompt the viewer to mediate on the relationship between the human and the divine. In fact, he leads the observer through an ascending path, beginning with the skeleton set at its base – symbol of human frailty, as also underscored by the inscription: IO FU GIÀ QUEL CHE VOI SETE: E QUEL CHI SON VOI ANCOR SARETE (I have already been that which you are and that which I am you are yet to be). The eyes then ascend through the figures of the Lenzi family who commissioned the work, to the Virgin and Saint John, to reach Christ crucified, above which God the Father appears. Masaccio, complying to the perspective rules of scenic construction, represents in the donors' figures in the background in the same proportions as those of the sacred characters, thus charging the hierarchical symbolism between the terrestrial and the transcendent with wholly Humanist significance.

SANTA TRINITA

A romanesque church was founded on this site by the Vallombrosan Order in the second half the 11th Century. The interior façade with its large oculus, suspended arches and crypt, is all that remain of that church today. In the mid-12th Century, Santa Trinita received the title of abbey and grew in importance, so much so, that in 1285 Cimabue's *Maestà* (p. 12) was set on the main altar. In the 14th Century it was given its current gothic arrangement and enlarged through addition of the side chapels. These were further modified and decorated beginning in the 15th Century, for example, the Bartolini Salimbeni Chapel (fourth on the right aisle), where between 1420 and 1425 Lorenzo Monaco frescoed *Stories of the Virgin* over an earlier decoration by Spinello Aretino (partly uncovered during restoration), while at the same time, Lorenzo Ghiberti was painting the Strozzi Chapel, now the sacristy. The Sassetti Chapel bears Domenico Ghirlandaio's masterpiece, *Saint Francis bringing a child back to life*, in which the façade's original appearance can be seen, that is, before Bernardo Buontalenti's late 16th-century modifications. Buontalenti, who also remodelled the presbytery and convent, designed the current pietra forte façade. Since 1671 the miraculous *Crucifix* by Giovanni Gualberto, originally from San Miniato al Monte, has been kept in the first chapel to the right of the main chapel.

GIULIANO DA SANGALLO
(architecture and tombs of Francesco and Nera Sassetti)

DOMENICO GHIRLANDAIO
(frescoes and altarpiece)
1483-1485
Right transept, second chapel to the right of the main chapel, Sassetti Chapel

Francesco Sassetti, a close friend of the Medici family and administrator of the their bank offices in Geneva and later Lyon, commissioned Ghirlandaio with decorating his family chapel. The chapel itself was designed by the architect Giuliano da Sangallo, who adapted the existing gothic arrangement to fifteenth-century styles and also carried out the porphyry sarcophagi of Francesco and Nera Sassetti and overlying ornamental arches. The fresco cycle, one of the most beautiful of the 15th Century, was carried out between 1483 and 1485. Ghirlandaio mixes elements from classical antiquity, such as the *Sibyls* on the vault, with representations of sacred events, such as the *Adoration of the shepherds* in the splendid altar panel of Flemish inspiration, and the *Scenes of the Life of Saint Francis* that represents the central theme developed on the chapel walls. The choice of such subjects was very much dictated by Sassetti's belonging to the cultured ambience of the Medici entourage, which certainly influenced the figurative design. Two of the episodes were set in prestigious locations, in Piazza della Signoria

and outside Santa Trinita, where the rich and famous of the time were sure to behold them, including the Medici and the scholars, Agnolo Poliziano and Luigi Pulci. The scenes unfold in a happy narrative vein, pervaded by a sense of serenity and balance, almost as if to hint at a return to the golden age of the Medici, who had made Florence the Athens of the modern world.

Domenico Ghirlandaio,
Adoration of the Shepherds

LUCA DELLA ROBBIA

Tomb of Benozzo Federighi
1454-1456
Left transept, second chapel to the left of the main chapel

The sepulchre of the Bishop of Fiesole, Benozzo Federighi, was Luca della Robbia's last marble monument. It was transferred here from the northern transept of the church of San Pancrazio, which was destroyed, and lost its tall plinth with red marble panelling in the process. In conformity with the deceased bishop's character, the sarcophagus's design is austere and formally simple, a feature further accented by the loss of the gilding that once covered the decoration and fabrics. In contrast, the lively majolica frame bears small paintings of fruit and flowers whose delicate colour blendings make them stand out from the gilded background.

SANTISSIMA ANNUNZIATA

The origins of the church of the Annunciation date back to 1250, when seven noble Florentines, devotees of the Virgin who called themselves the "servants of Mary", retreated to do penitence at Monte Senario near Florence. Upon their return to the city their numbers increased, and the nascent Order of the Servites had a small oratory built. The following century saw increasing devotion to the miraculous image of the *Annunciation* preserved in the church, which was enlarged accordingly. The building reached its current dimensions between 1444 and 1477, during which time Michelozzo began the gallery with chapels arranged in a crown around the apse, finished by Leon Battista Alberti. The hemispherical cupola was then added with a single casting of concrete, following a Roman technique. The church underwent further modifications in the 17th Century, the first years of which saw the building of the portico on the square. The inside took on a lavish, typically baroque aspect: arches and pillars were covered with precious marbles, and the ceiling opulently sculpted and gilded. Between 1664 and 1670 the painting of the *Assumption* by Volterrano (also author of the cupola frescoes in the gallery) was placed here. The intervals between the windows hold panels of the *Miracles of Maria Annunziata* (the same theme found in the medallions overlying the arched entrance to the chapels). In 1704 the gallery was modified by Giovan Battista Foggini, who also designed the high altar.

Chiostrino dei Voti

The Cloister of the Ex-votos was built together with the convent, though it was restructured in the mid-15th Century by Michelozzo and decorated with frescos between 1461 and 1517. In the 17th Century it was given over to receiving the votive offerings of the faithful to the Madonna. The oldest of the frescoes is the *Adoration of the Shepherds*, on the left side of the entrance, painted by Alessio Baldovinetti with minute precision, especially in the landscape. However, it is difficult to appreciate the intricacy of the work because of the loss of much of the paint (owing to the dry fresco technique used). The next fresco depicts *Stories of Saint Phillip Benizzi*, the Saint-General of the Servite order. The earliest story of the saint, the *Vocation*, was painted by Cosimo Rosselli in 1474; the other five were entrusted to Andrea del Sarto who, well aware of the contemporaneous work of Fra Bartolomeo, da Vinci and Raphael, quickly completed it between 1509 and 1510 in order to insure himself a prestigious position. Del Sarto returned to work in the cloister in 1511 to paint the monumental *Coming of the Magi* in the lunette to the right of the entranceway, and once again in 1514 for the *Birth of Mary* in the last lunette on the right wall. On this same wall his workshop companion, Franciabigio, frescoed the *Marriage of Mary* in 1513. Lastly, his young pupils were given the task of finishing the cycle devoted to the Virgin: Pontormo with his tender *Visitation* (1514 to 1516) and Rosso Fiorentino, the restless *Assumption* (1517), in the last lunette near the entrance.

BACCIO BANDINELLI

Dead Christ supported by Nicodemus
1554-1560
Right side of church,
Chapel of Pietà, to the right of the crossing

Baccio Bandinelli was one of the most gifted sculptors at the Medici court and author of *Hercules and Cacus* opposite the copy of Michelangelo's *David* (p. 36) in front of Palazzo Vecchio. The Pazzi family, who had owned the small chapel to the right of the main chapel since its beginnings in the 14th Century, granted it to the artist, who decided to set up his family's sepulchre there. Therefore, in 1554 he began sculpting the life-size marble group with Christ compassionately sustained by Nicodemus, whose countenance is a self-portrait of the sculptor. He depicted himself once again on the back of the statue's base, together with his wife, Giacoma. He had planned to complete the decoration of the altar with Saint John and Saint Catherine of Siena, but died before beginning the work.

ANDREA DEL CASTAGNO

The Holy Trinity with Saint Jerome
1454
Third chapel to the left,
Chapel of Saint Jerome

The chapel, frescoed entirely by Alessandro Allori in the mid 16th Century, held an altarpiece of the *Last Judgement* (now visible in the adjacent chapel), a clear homage to Michelangelo, that covered the underlying fresco by Andrea del Castagno, discovered only at the end of the 19th Century. The fresco was probably commissioned from the painter by the Company of Saint Jerome – one of the nearly one hundred lay fraternities active in Florence during the 15th Century – which met near Santissima Annunziata. Through innovative iconography, it represents *Penitent Saint Jerome* wearing the grey tunic held at the waist by a sash , such as that worn by the order of Saint Jerome up to 1460. Nearly ten years after his completing the refectory of Sant'Apollonia (p. 179), Andrea del Castagno reasserts his rigorous use of perspective in the foreshortening of the metal-like haloes of the saints and especially the Crucifix above.

Cappella dell'Annunziata
In the nave against the interior façade

According to church legends, the miraculous image of the *Annunciation* was found in the original oratory building in the mid-13th Century. Instead, stylistic considerations lead to a more recent dating, sometime in the 14th Century. In order to safeguard this venerated treasure, in the mid 15th Century, Piero de' Medici decided to erect a marble shrine that was to become the focal point for popular devotion. The tabernacle was designed by Michelozzo, who had already created a similar one on commission to this same Medici at San Miniato al Monte (p. 151), and carried out by Pagno di Lapo Portigiani, the architect's loyal collaborator. A partition was set up to enclose the shrine and decorated with bronze rose windows, in turn closed off by a bronze lattice-work in a cord motif by Maso di Bartolomeo. The shrines commemorative function became even more explicit in 1600, when Ferdinando I donated the silver palio, or banner, bearing his portrait, so as to attest to the bond between the cult of the Madonna and that of the Medici family. With time, the precious offerings became ever more numerous, so much so as to almost completely obscure the structure of the tabernacle, covered in the 17th Century with a wooden canopy.

ANDREA DEL SARTO

Madonna del Sacco

1525
Large Cloister (Chiostro dei Morti), above the entranceway to the church

Andrea del Sarto, who had already left significant works in the Servite church (p. 169) completes this fresco at the peak of his classicism. The balanced, solemn composition in the lunette, framed by architecture and painted in foreshortening to be viewed from below, depicts figures with a monumental quality reminiscent of Michelangelo and Raphael. It was very much admired "for its drawing, grace and beautiful colouring", as Vasari writes. The painting came to be known as *Madonna del Sacco* because of the sack under the reading Saint Joseph's arm, though it may actually represent an adoration or the flight to Egypt.

SANTO SPIRITO

In the mid 13th Century the Augustinians, a mendicant order engaged in the apostolate, settled in the area and became an important cultural point of reference for city residents. In the late 14th Century a new church was needed, and its design was entrusted to Filippo Brunelleschi, who delivered the plan only in 1436, the year the Cathedral dome was vaulted. The original design called for a façade facing the Arno River. However, as this would have involved demolishing a number of houses on that side, the plan was met with fierce opposition and was therefore never carried out. This was not the only modification made to the original project: upon the unexpected death of the architect in 1446 (two years after work had begun), his student, Antonio Manetti took over, followed then by Salvi d'Andrea, both of whom made a number of changes to the façade and dome, as well as the semicircular chapels, which were supposed to remain visible and impart a curving line to the church's external perimeter. In 1471 a fire broke out in the still functioning old church abutting the nascent new one, and little was saved of its furnishings: the fourteenth-century polyptych by Maso di Banco remains on an altar to the right in the main crossing. Harmony, equilibrium and compositional clarity – highlighted by the grey *pietra serena*, white plaster and terracotta floor – characterise the church interior, awash in diffuse lighting attenuated at the side aisles. The Latin cross arrangement, elongated at the transept, combines a centre plan with that of a Basilica. Brunelleschi's influence is clearly perceptible in the sacristy and vestibule, designed by Giuliano da Sangallo sometime before 1490.

FILIPPINO LIPPI

Madonna and Child with young Saint John, Saints and donors ("Pala Nerli")
circa 1494
Right transept, Nerli Chapel

This altarpiece, still kept in its original location in the Nerli Chapel, is the work of Filippino Lippi who also designed a stain-glass window for the chapel, now lost. It was painted in about 1494, during the same years when the artist was frescoing the Carafa Chapel in Santa Maria sopra Minerva in Rome. In fact, many of its elements are drawn from antiquity, such as the decoration of the throne and pillars. The donors, Nanna di Neri Capponi and Tanai Nerli are in the foreground. Patron of the arts, Tanai Nerli held important offices in the Florentine Signoria. The scene in the background takes place near the Florentine Porta San Frediano and shows Tanai in front of his building in Borgo San Jacopo greeting his young daughter. It seems to allude to the diplomatic mission that he carried out in November of 1494.

Intent on conquest, King Charles VIII of France had amassed his army at Pisa, and Nerli was sent to meet the king and try to dissuade him from his course. Nerli returned victorious from that enterprise on Saint Martin's day and, in fact, an agreement between the Florentine Republic and the sovereign was signed shortly thereafter, on Saint Catherine's day. Hence, the presence of the two saints by the enthroned Virgin with Child aims to immortalise that glorious moment.

ANDREA SANSOVINO
Altar of the Sacrament
circa 1492
Left transept, Corbinelli Chapel

From 1485 up to the early 17th Century, when the high altar was finally built, the Corbinelli family had the privilege of guarding the Sacrament in their own chapel. Thus, desirous of a suitable marble altar, they commissioned the sculpture from Andrea Sansovino, who had already worked on the church sacristy. The original structure, aspiring to classical models redolent of Roman triumphal arches, was enlarged only a few years later, following Sansovino's design, with marble facing divided by pilasters in imitation of the wooden choir backs. The 17th Century saw the addition of the baluster, crowning and doors of the ciborium. The iconography is linked to the body of Christ held within: in fact, the *Pietà* is shown in the palio, while the *Last Supper* is in the centre of the predella; above, the *Annunciation* and *Coronation* refer to the mystery of *Christ's Incarnation*. The tabernacle is surrounded by Saint Matthew on the left, his martyrdom below, and Saint James with the miracle of Hermogenes, to the right.

MICHELANGELO BUONARROTI
Crucifix
1492-1493

This wooden *Crucifix* was discovered in the convent of Santo Spirito in 1962. The paint covering, added perhaps between the 18th and 19th Centuries, was stripped away and the work was fully restored to reveal its extraordinariness. It was thus identified as the crucifix commissioned from Michelangelo by the prior of Santo Spirito, Nicolaio di Giovanni di Lapo Bicchiellini, between 1492 and 1493. It was kept above the church's main altar up to the early 17th Century, when the altar was dismantled and replaced by the current one. The *Crucifix* (the original cross was replaced in the 19th Century) is clearly a descendent of the 14th-15th century sacred tradition, though the stately and delicate body structure reveals the innovative elements introduced by Michelangelo, perhaps adhering to Fra Girolamo Savonarola's conception of the most suitable representation of the Crucifix – one that melds human corporeality with religious fervour.

REFECTORIES

CENACOLO "DI FULIGNO"

PIETRO PERUGINO

Last Supper
circa 1490
Convent of Sant'Onofrio,
refectory, currently a museum

From 1419 the convent of Sant'Onofrio in via Faenza hosted a congregation of Franciscan nuns established by two noblewomen from the town of Foligno in Umbria, hence the name by which it is known. Pietro Perugino was entrusted with frescoing the refectory (cenacolo) with the *Last Supper* over an older version. The painter, also from Umbria, was famous throughout Italy and ran a flourishing workshop in Florence from 1482 to 1492. By now, the refectory is universally recognised as his own work, though it had long remained unknown due the strict seclusion observed by the nuns. In fact, it was discovered only after suppression of the convent in the early 19th Century and was immediately attributed to Perugino's brilliant student, Raphael. However, the typical elements of Perugino's work are evident: the countryside of the *Oration in the Garden*, the parvis with the exquisitely adorned monochromic pilasters, the delicate chromatic range and the style of the heads of the Franciscan saints in the tondi and Christ with the apostles identified by theirs names on the platform plinth. The apostles sit on cloth-covered wooden benches round a u-shaped table with Judas isolated in the foreground side of the table, as dictated by traditional iconography.

CENACOLO DI OGNISSANTI

DOMENICO
GHIRLANDAIO

Last Supper
1480
Convent of Ognissanti,
refectory, currently a museum

The refectory opens onto the first cloister, built between 1561 and 1580. The refectory it-self was constructed in 1480, the date over the entranceway on the interior façade, as well as in the fresco with the *Last Supper*, which Domenico Ghirlandaio painted shortly after the one in San Marco (p. 83). The illusion of a virtual extension to real space is imparted by the false loggia opening onto an airy garden with palms and cypresses (respectively al-luding to martyrdom and death) orange trees and cedars (symbols of Heaven) and birds in flight (also linked to Christian iconography). However, beyond the symbolism, the atten-tion to particulars, clearly of Flemish inspiration, is immediate to the eye. One can discern the bright cherries and oranges, the contents of the glasses and bottles on the embroidered tablecloth, and the emblem of Ognissanti (OSSCI, Omnes sancti) on the tray and brass pitch-er by the wooden bench, as well as on the rose-filled white ceramic vase. The apostles are seated two-by-two, according to the ancient custom of sharing a plate. Their dynamic pos-es express the naturalness of the ongoing dialogue and set them in life-like relationship to the observer. Following the 1966 flood, the fresco detached, and the sinopie are now on display in the refectory.

CENACOLO DI SAN SALVI

ANDREA DEL SARTO

Last Supper
1511-1527
Convent of San Michele a San
Salvi, refectory, currently a
museum

The Vallombrosan convent was founded in the mid-11th Century, and subsequently enlarged and adorned with masterpieces such as the *Baptism of Christ* by Verrocchio and da Vinci, now in the Uffizi (p. 24). As the great refectory was to serve the function of welcoming guests, the monk Don Ilario Panichi had it placed on the southern side of the second cloister, so that it would have a separate entrance directly accessible from the road. In 1511 he entrusted its decoration to Andrea del Sarto, who began the fresco with five tondi in a band under the arch on the back wall, so as to create the illusion of a niche. In the centre he painted the Trinity, adopting an iconography seldom seen in Italy, while to the sides he set the four guardians of the Vallombrosan order. The tondi are surrounded by a decoration in grotesques, executed in all probability by Andrea di Cosimo Feltrini, a painter very skilled in this genre. These portraits testify to the work of Andrea del Sarto in his early years – those immediately following his *Stories of Saint Phillip* in the Chiostrino dei Voti in Santissima Annunziata (p. 169) when he was still very much influenced by Fra Bartolomeo (the painter that dominated Florentine art in the first decade of the 16th Century). On the other hand, the *Last Supper*, frescoed in about 1526-1527 represents the artist's mature years. It is set in an interior whose pavement is depicted in perspective, with an open balcony above showing two servants. The apostles are seated around Christ in the centre of the table which the fills the full width of the painting. The gestural and facial expressiveness of the characters in their ample iridescent robes enliven the solemn scene, interrupted by the marble panelling.

CENACOLO DI SANT'APOLLONIA

ANDREA DEL CASTAGNO

Last Supper, Deposition, Crucifixion, Resurrection

circa 1447
Convent of Sant'Apollonia,
refectory, currently a museum

It is not known who commissioned the frescoing of the refectory of the Benedictine convent of Sant'Apollonia. Due to the nun's strict seclusion, until the 19th Century the interior had never been studied. In 1860 the monastery was suppressed, restored and transformed into a museum in 1891. Restorations revealed the three painted-over scenes of the *Passion*. In the cardinal central section, Andrea del Castagno depicted the traditional theme of the *Crucifixion*, while he placed the *Resurrection* to the left and *Deposition* to the right. The various scenes are separated by two scalloped windows, though united by the background landscape and the six angels in flight. Christ is represented beardless, and the episodes unfold in the light of day betokening salvation in an illusory outdoor space created behind the room where the *Last Supper* is under way. The true novelty of this refectory is, in fact, its perspective. The rigour of its application makes the architectural structure of the marble inlaid room reminiscent of Leon Battista Alberti. References to the ancient world, common amongst Renaissance artists, are in the pilasters and the superb sphinxes on the bench. Bearded Christ presides over the supper, surrounded by the apostles, draped in lush, heavy robes, in heroic poses and with faces boldly drawn in *chiaroscuro*.

CENACOLO DI SANTO SPIRITO

ANDREA DI CIONE (KNOWN AS ORCAGNA)

Last Supper, Crucifixion
circa 1367-1368
Convent of Santo Spirito,
ancient refectory, currently a
museum of the Romano
Foundation

The refectory houses the Museum of the Romano Foundation which holds the works donated by this Neapolitan antiquarian to Florence, including sculptures by Tino di Camaino and Donatello. The room, the only one in the Augustinian convent to preserve its original architecture, was built in the mid 14th Century. It is a large rectangular hall with large windows along its length and a niche pulpit for reading. After the 1866 suppression of the order, it suffered serious damage, particularly, the opening of a door in the wall bearing the *Last Supper*, which destroyed nearly all of it. In fact, only two apostles remain, flanked by an Augustinian saint, while above, the *Crucifixion* has been damaged in its lower central part. The great painting, one of the largest frescoes surviving from the 14th Century, belongs to the late period (1367-1368.) of Orcagna and his workshop. It was commissioned, as can be seen from the coat of arms in the decorative band, by the Cambi di Napoleone family. The spatial design is elementary, and the narrative style is didactic in its connotations.

CHIOSTRO DELLO SCALZO

ANDREA DEL SARTO AND
FRANCIABIGIO

*Stories of Saint John the
Baptist* and *The Virtues*
1510-1526

The rectangular cloister with funeral symbols on the slender columns' plinths gets its name from the lay association, Compagnia dei Disciplinati, devoted to Saint John the Baptist, whose seat was housed here from the end of the 15th Century. The fraternity was in fact called "Lo Scalzo" (the Barefoot), because during processions the cross bearer would walk shoeless. Andrea del Sarto was entrusted with decorating the walls in 1510. He worked uninterruptedly on the monochrome *Stories of Saint John the Baptist* and *the Virtues* until 1526, except for his 1518-1519 stay in France at the court of François I, when Franciabigio did the *Benediction of Saint Zacharias* and *Saint John meeting Christ*. Such a long interval of time embraces practically the whole of Andrea del Sarto's stylistic evolution, from the early *Baptism of Christ*, to the *Baptism of the multitude* clearly showing da Vinci and Michelangelo's influence, and finally the eclectic formulation of the *Birth of Saint John*.

PALACES

PALAZZO CORSINI

In 1656 Bartolomeo Corsini began the work of restructuring the family buildings on via del Parione. Alfonso Parigi was the first to supervise the work, followed by Ferdinando Tacca, and finally Pier Francesco Silvani in 1679, who is credited with the main building's unusual U-shape, as well as the helical staircase and the second façade whose loggias and terraces overlook the river. Instead, it was Antonio Ferri who created the grand staircase leading to the throne room, which was decorated by Anton Domenico Gabbiani with statues and the vault frescoes with the apotheosis of the Corsini house. The throne room leads to the other luxurious halls exhibiting the family painting collection, initiated in 1765 by don Lorenzo Corsini, nephew and namesake of pope Clement XII. The collection is particularly rich in 17th and 18th-century paintings, even if earlier works are not lacking. It is therefore a private collection strictly linked to the baroque building that houses it.

PALAZZO DAVANZATI

The building, a rare example of the homes of the Florentine nobility, was built by the Davizzi in the mid-14th Century. Its subsequent owners, the Bartolini, sold it to the Davanzati family in 1578. After the last descendant of the Davanzati committed suicide, the building was subjected to many remodellings, from which it was spared in 1904 when it was acquired by the antiquarian Elia Volpi. It then changed hands a number of times before being opened to the public as the Museum of the ancient Florentine House in 1956. The sandstone façade, divided by the string-course frames, has three tiers of windows overlying that which was once an open loggia with three reduced arches. The covered roof terrace was added in the 16th Century, as was the large Davanzati coat of arms. The façade bears ring hooks for hitching horses, as well as long bars, called erri, for hanging laundry or treasured cloth articles. The courtyard is dominated by galleries and a flying buttress staircase which provides access to the upper floor. Parts of the interior maintain their original wall decorations. Apart from paintings and sculptures, the rooms display majolicas, household items and other furnishings that testify to day-to-day life in an ancient Florentine home.

PALAZZO MEDICI-RICCARDI

Built between 1444 and 1462 by the architect Michelozzo for Cosimo de' Medici, this building can be considered the prototype of late 15th-century Florentine nobleman's home. The arrangement of the rusticated façade is classically renaissance: the protrusion of the blocks varies from thickest in the lower tier, decreasing on the first floor, to become a smooth facing on the second. The rounded windows are divided into double lancets, and the imposing overhanging eaves frame the construction above. The square courtyard in the interior contains columns and arches on the ground floor, double lancet windows on the first and a covered loggia on the second. In 1517 the building was subjected its earliest modifications by

Michelangelo, who closed the small loggia that once stood at the corner of via Gori and via Cavour, and replaced it with large "inginocchiate" windows, that is, "kneeling" on large protruding ledge sills. In 1659 the building was acquired by the Riccardi family, who first had a new wing built on via de' Ginori, then in 1685 added a new staircase and state rooms by extending the façade on via Cavour according to a project by Giovan Battista Foggini. This same architect-sculptor created the opulent Gallery destined to hold the gems, medals and bronze work of the family collection. The gallery's rich plaster decoration and vault frescoes are by Luca Giordano.

185

Chapel of the Magi

Set in the heart of the Medici-Riccardi building, this elegant little chapel is the building's most intimate and private spot. Between 1459 and 1462, Benozzo Gozzoli frescoed the fable-like *Procession of the Magi* on commission to Piero il Gottoso, the son of Cosimo il Vecchio. In honour of the periodic street processions organised by the Company of the Magi under the auspices of the Medici, Gozzoli, Beato Angelico's pupil, transposes the chronological setting of the Adoration of the Magi. The procession, in fact, depicts numerous exponents of the Medici house on a background showing the hills surrounding Florence. However, the scenes are also replete with characters in oriental costumes, such as the emperor Giovanni Palelologo, portrayed as one of the Magi. These are likely the distant echoes of the processions in which young Benozzo took part, together with the most eminent religious and political personalities of the Eastern Empire, twenty years prior, on the occasion of the Council that ended the Schism with the East. The chapel has a beautiful lacunar ceiling of carved and painted wood, fine marble intarsia pavement, the work of Michelozzo, and choir stalls designed by Giuliano da Sangallo, which were added in 1469. The altar contains the panel of the *Adoration of the Child* by pseudo Pier Francesco Fiorentino.

PALAZZO RUCELLAI

If the architects preferred by the Medici were Brunelleschi and Michelozzo, the powerful Rucellai family name is inextricably linked to Leon Battista Alberti. A friend of Giovanni Rucellai, Alberti worked above all on building this, the family town mansion, though he would later dedicate himself to designing the façade of the church of Santa Maria Novella (p. 163), and finally the chapel adjoining the church of San Pancrazio (now the Marino Marini Museum) with the shrine of the Holy Sepulchre. This building in via della Vigna, actually formed from the union of two constructions, was completed in various stages from 1455 to 1458 and 1465 to 1470 by Bernardo Rossellino, following Alberti's design. Due to the structures' irregularity, heavy modifications were called for, especially in the façade. The incomplete right section of the façade reveals how the construction, originally designed as a smaller, single-entrance building, has been enlarged through addition of a new portal. Moreover, in order to re-establish its symmetry, two more bays had to be added to the original five. In the façade Alberti applies the classical architectural scheme of layered storeys in a horizontal layout defined by string-courses and vertical partitions imparted by pilasters with intervening double lancet windows. Viewed as the light plays on its profile, the refined whole produces an intense chiaroscuro effect, very unlike fourteenth-century architectural conceptions.

PALAZZO STROZZI

In 1460 the Strozzi family returned to Florence from the exile to which the hostile Medici had banished them. In 1489 Filippo il Vecchio, the most illustrious of the Strozzi, acquired some small property and began erecting the building that would celebrate his family's exploits. Although traditionally attributed to Benedetto da Maiano, the building is actually the fruit of Maiano's collaboration with Simone del Pollaiolo, known as Cronaca. Benedetto furnished the design and supervised the work up to the first floor, while Cronaca took over direction of the stone-cutters in 1489, realising both the richly decorated eaves framing the building above and the spacious elegant courtyard in the interior. The plan was however never completed, and the building is lacking the southern façade and part of its eaves. It is a perfect cube with three rusticated stone façades whose ashlar work smooths out in the upper storeys. Each side has a wide entranceway, and the four corners bear wrought iron flag clamps and chandeliers, forged after Benedetto da Maiano's design by Niccolò Grosso, known as Caparra.

FORTE BELVEDERE

Immediately above the thirteenth-century Porta San Giorgio city gate looms Fort Belvedere, named so because of the spectacular view it offers of the city and surrounding countryside. Ferdinando I de' Medici had it built between 1589 and 1591 by Bernardo Buontalenti. Don Giovanni de' Medici made some modifications on the eastern slope of Boboli Gardens, to which the fortress is now linked so that the grand duke's family residing at Pitti Palace could retreat here. The fortifications are made up of two anterior ramparts and two tenailles with five bastions. The villa in its centre was designed by Bartolomeo Ammannati in the 1570s. Therefore, the villa was already standing when the fortress was constructed, after which Buontalenti modified its subterranean quarters to hold the Medici treasures.

ITINERARIES

The religious centre

The religious heart of Florence is the monument complex of the Cathedral with Giotto's bell tower, the Baptistery and the many other buildings surrounding piazza del Duomo and contiguous piazza di San Giovanni. Here you will find, on the western side, the archiepiscopal seat, then on the corner of via de' Calzaiuoli, the Bigallo building with its loggia, which originally housed the Company of the same name devoted to the care of orphans, and finally at no. 19, the Arciconfraternità della Misericordia (Brotherhood of Mercy) dedicated to aiding the ill. This is the first itinerary; it is here that any visitor must set out to discover Florence. In Roman times and the Late Middle Ages this area was actually at the limits of Florence's inhabited area. However, the last ring of city walls (1284-1333) delimited it as the town centre, which grew to become the heart of the city's Christian community as well. In fact, while the Baptistery with its bronze doors and mosaics is an exhortation to theological reflection, the bell tower with its decoration recounts the fate of Mankind, and the Cathedral of Santa Maria del Fiore dominates the city skyline with Brunelleschi's cupola, which, in the words of another great Renaissance architect, Leon Battista Alberti, is so "broad as to cast its shadow over all Tuscan peoples". No tour of the centre is complete without a visit to the Museo dell'Opera del Duomo whose entrance is behind the cathedral apse at no. 9. The Museum holds many of the works originally carried out for the Baptistery, the Cathedral's façade and interior, as well as the bell tower.

The centres of political power

ORSANMICHELE (P. 144) – PALAZZO VECCHIO (P. 126) – DIOCESAN MUSEUM OF SANTO STEFANO AL PONTE (P. 87)– BARGELLO NATIONAL MUSEUM (P. 90) – BADIA FIORENTINA (P. 134)

From piazza del Duomo, we cross via de' Calzaiuoli, widened during the urban development of the late 19th Century; on the right between via Orsanmichele and via de' Lamberti is the imposing structure of Orsanmichele, the headquarters of the powerful Arti, or Guilds, who decorated its outside with niches to hold the statues of their patron saints. We then come to piazza della Signoria, which represented the seat of civil power beginning in the late 13th Century with construction of the Palazzo dei Priori, a building that would change its name many times over the years, to be dubbed at last Palazzo Vecchio (i.e., the Old Building) in the late 16th Century, when the grand duke's court moved from here to its new residence at Pitti Palace. The square's current arrangement is the result of centuries of changes and additions. In particular, between 1376 and 1382, the Loggia dei Priori in front of Palazzo Vecchio was built, probably on a project by Andrea di Cione, known as Orcagna, in order to provide shelter to the city's illustrious personages during public ceremonies. It was therefore a building linked to the history of the Florentine republic, a fact not lost upon Cosimo I de' Medici, who, after taking up residence in Palazzo Vecchio in 1541, transformed the loggia into a garrison for the Lanzi – that is, the Swiss and German mercenaries in the service of the Medici – thereby giving rise to its alternative appellative of "Loggia dei Lanzi". Shortly thereafter, in 1545 Benvenuto Cellini's statue of *Perseus* was placed here (currently under restoration), followed in 1583 by the *Rape of the Sabine Women* by Giambologna (under the right

arcade); thus, the loggia progressively became an open-air sculpture exhibition. The bronze equestrian monument of Cosimo I is also by Giambologna, who moreover collaborated with Bartolomeo Ammannati and other artists on the 1575 *Fountain of Neptune*, which celebrates the maritime ambitions of Cosimo I. Many masterpieces have been set before Palazzo Vecchio as symbols of the various governments which rose to power: *Judith and Holofernes* by Donatello, Michelangelo's *David*, now both copies of the originals kept respectively in Palazzo Vecchio and the Gallery of the Accademia, and *Hercules* and *Cacus* by Baccio Bandinelli. From here, just few steps brings you to the building's interior, where its monumental quarters can be visited. After returning to the square, you should take a detour through the narrow medieval alleyways, through Chiasso de' Baroncelli to the right of the Loggia dei Priori and then once again right into via Lambertesca, then left under an arch to reach the small square of piazzetta di Santo Stefano al Ponte, the deconsecrated church whose lower portions are covered by a splendid Romanesque façade. To the right, in the ex-convent, is the Diocesan Museum, holding an important painting by Giotto. From piazza della Signoria, by following via de' Gondi along the left side of Palazzo Vecchio, you can observe the signs of the various stages of its construction: the original cube by Arnolfo di Cambio and the subsequent addition of the Hall of the High Council, destined to be transformed by Vasari into the Salone dei Cinquecento in the same period that the building was extended toward via dei Leoni. We then come to piazza San Firenze, in which stands Palazzo Gondi, begun by Giuliano da Sangallo in 1490, and opposite, the late baroque façade of the complex of San Firenze, most of which is taken up by the large courthouse, except for the still functioning church of San Filippo on the extreme left. A bit further along, at the entrance of via del Proconsolo, is the Badia Fiorentina, a Benedictine abbey founded in 978, and the Palazzo del Capitano del Popolo, the first building in Florence established as a permanent city institution and destined to house the Bargello, the important national museum with precious works of sculpture and the applied arts.

The jewel case of masterpieces

THE UFFIZI (P. 10-11)

Visiting the Uffizi signifies taking a journey through the absolute masterpieces of modern Europe's oldest museum – one of the world's most important for its collection of 13th to 18th-century Italian and European painting. It is therefore an undertaking that requires, yes, time (some of which can be saved by booking in advance), but most of all, the right frame of mind: the art work contained here is such that it may induce a sense of light-headedness. To the right of Palazzo Vecchio, toward the river, is the piazzale degli Uffizi, an elongated square whose spatial arrangement is mid-way between that of a courtyard, a square and a street, delimited by the three wings of the Uffizi building begun by Vasari in 1560. Five years later Vasari would add the corridor uniting Palazzo Vecchio to the new court residence at Pitti Palace. The corridor's first section is visible on via della Ninna, between Palazzo Vecchio and the Uffizi. On the right side of the same street parts of the Romanesque church of San Pier Scheraggio, which was engulfed by the Uffizi, are still visible, including its wall and the columns of the left aisle destroyed in 1410 in order to widen the road. Since 1835 twenty-eight statues of illustrious Tuscans have occupied the niches within the loggia's pillars. Under the left portico is the entrance to the ever-expanding gallery. The Contini Bonacossi collection is held here and will be visible in the near future in the museum's interior, as also the displays in the Loggia overlooking the Arno, prepared with archaeological finds. It is, in fact, from the short wing of the Uffizi that, following the perspective imparted by the Uffizi's long axis, one looks out on the wonderful panorama made up of the massive structure of Palazzo della Signoria, the statue-laden communal square before it and, further beyond, the dome of Santa Maria del Fiore, mimicking the gentile profile of the hills on the other side of the river. The course of the Vasarian corridor, the elevated passage created for the private use of the duke and his entourage, can be traced as it winds its way from the west wing of the Uffizi on massive arch structures on the Arno, and crosses Ponte Vecchio to continue its course up to Pitti Palace. In certain periods of the year, decided upon by the arts and cultural authorities, one may book a tour through the corridor to admire the self-portraits of the painters that are on display here. At the end of the third corridor, where the Medici once listened to music in the hanging gardens above the Loggia della Signoria, there is a spectacular view of the underlying square.

The Santa Croce quarter

This itinerary covers the area dominated by the Franciscan Basilica of Santa Croce, a city quarter set opposite and symmetrical to that of Santa Maria Novella. When the first Franciscan monks arrived here in 1228, only two years after Saint Francis's death, the terrain was marshy. The course of the Arno was then diverted to reclaim the land, and new city walls made to enclosed the growing wool manufacturing district that had grown up around the already expanding church. Arnolfo di Cambio, the town's most sought after architect during the late 13th Century, was given the charge of planning the new church of Santa Croce, today one of the most visited sites in Florence because of the tombs of the many illustrious men found here, as well as its fourteenth-century frescoes, including those by Giotto. To the church's right is the entrance to the Museo dell'Opera di Santa Croce, whose refectory, designed by Taddeo Gaddi, holds *Saint Louis of Toulouse* by Donatello and the *Crucifix* by Cimabue, while at the back of the cloister is Brunelleschi's jewel of renaissance art, the Pazzi Chapel. Returning to the square, which has hosted festivals and games since the 14th Century, and still today is the site of ancient-style football matches, we take Borgo Santa Croce on the left, whose oblique course out of the square leads to via de' Benci. Turning left we reach Palazzo Corsi at no. 6, acquired in the early 20th Century by Herbert Percy Horne, who amassed his own collection here, transforming it into "the noble residence of the cultured, affluent renaissance man". After a visit to the museum, go right on via de' Benci, and about half way up, turn left under an arch to come out into piazza dei Peruzzi, where the building of the powerful banker family of the same name was built in the late 13th Century on the ruins of a Roman amphitheatre, whose perimeter it follows. Returning to via de' Benci and continuing up to piazza Santa Croce, at the crossroads of via dell'Anguillara, you will find the fifteenth-century Palazzo Cocchi-Serristori (no. 1) by Giuliano da Sangallo, and on the southern side, Palazzo dell'Antella (no. 20-22), whose façade was frescoed from 1619 to 1621 under the direction of Giovanni da San Giovanni. The itinerary continues along side the church of Santa Croce in via San Giuseppe, then left into via delle Pinzochere, to come out in via Ghibellini in front of the Casa Buonarroti Museum (no. 70), once Michelangelo's home, which, apart from containing two of his masterpieces, is a tribute to his family's history.

The Santa Maria Novella quarter

The bell tower and apse of Santa Maria Novella are immediately visible just opposite the Main Railway Station, Stazione Centrale di Santa Maria Novella, a work of rationalist architecture carried out between 1933 and 1935 by the Gruppo Toscano under the direction of Giovanni Michelucci. Santa Maria Novella is a Dominican church orientated in a symmetrical, though opposite position to the Franciscan church of Santa Croce, on the other side of the old town. Crossing via degli Avelli (i.e., Street of Tombs, so called because of the ogival sepulchres along the church's right side that continue into the square following the limits of an ancient cemetery), you reach the square dominated by the splendid façade of the church of Santa Maria Novella and, on the other side, by the loggia of the Spedale di San Paolo founded in the early 13th Century. The two veined marble obelisks resting on Giambologna's bronze turtles in the centre of the square mark the route followed by coaches during the racing competition, il Palio dei Cocchi. The race was instituted for the first time in 1563 by Cosimo I and was held every June 22, the eve of the feast of Saint John. After visiting the church and museum with its monumental cloisters, whose entrance is to the left of the façade, cross the square and either turn right at via della Scala al no. 16 to have a look at the ancient apothecary shop of Santa Maria Novella, or carry on straight to via de' Fossi, a street lined with antique shops, up to piazza Goldoni. Turn right here into Borgo Ognissanti to come to the church of Ognissanti, founded by the Franciscan order of the "Umiliati", a Lombard mendicant order that transformed the convent into a specialised wool manufacturing centre on the shores of the Arno River. The conventual complex, whose entrance is at no. 42, contains the refectory (cenacolo) frescoed with the *Last Supper* by Domenico Ghirlandaio.

The Medici

To understand the history of this powerful family whose destiny was so inextricably linked to Florence, one must begin with Palazzo Medici, the building later acquired by the Riccardi family and which today houses the Prefecture and provincial government offices. It is located in via Cavour, once called via Larga, a mandatory stop for visiting foreign dignitaries. Built by Michelozzo, it is the prototypical noble Florentine residence. The Medici lived here and made it the political and cultural centre of the city, from Cosimo il Vecchio to grand duke Cosimo I, who eventually moved the court residence to Palazzo della Signoria. The chapel, which can be visited at a charge by entering through the courtyard and ascending the staircase on the right, contains Benozzo Gozzoli's frescoes of the *Procession of the Magi*, evocative of the luxury of the Medici court. It was of course the Medici who financed Filippo Brunelleschi's project for the church of San Lorenzo. For three hundred years this basilica was to be the very embodiment of Medici rule – their royal chapel, where they would conduct their solemn family ceremonies and bury their dead. The artists called on to make their contributions were Brunelleschi, Donatello, Verrocchio, Michelangelo, that is to say, the maximum representatives of renaissance art. Once you have visited the church with the Old Sacristy, Cloister and Library, and picked you way through the colourful marketplace, enter the Museum of the Medici Chapels at piazza Madonna degli Aldobrandini no. 6. The Museum is actually part of the Basilica and includes, not only the Chapel of Princes, but Michelangelo's New Sacristy, as well. Lastly, take via Faenza to no. 40-42, to visit the refectory called the "Cenacolo di Fuligno" bearing the wonderful frescoes by Perugino.

The silence of the cloisters

Piazza San Marco is one of the liveliest squares in Florence. Yet, once you have crossed the threshold of the San Marco Museum (to the right of the church at no. 3), the hustle-bustle of contemporary life remains barred as you are immersed in the sombre atmosphere of the Dominican convent where time still seems regulated by prayer and study. Such is the serene harmony of Michelozzi's architecture and the deep spirituality of the frescoes and paintings by Beato Angelico, the painter monk who lived within these walls, as did Antonino Pierozzi, Girolamo Savonarola and Fra Bartolomeo. The museum visit includes the small refectory with the *Last Supper* frescoed by Domenico Ghirlandaio. Exiting on via della Dogana, to the left you reach via Cavour; here, after few paces to the right, is the entranceway to the Cloister know as "Chiostro dello Scalzo" (no. 69), famous for its frescoes by Andrea del Sarto and Franciabigio. Back once again on via Cavour, head back toward piazza San Marco, turn right into via Arazzieri and continue straight on to via XXVII Aprile, where you will find the entrance (no. 1) to the refectory of Sant'Apollonia that houses the museum devoted to Andrea del Castagno, who frescoed the rear wall of the refectory, applying the new, wholly renaissance rules of perspective.

Florence in the world's eye: Michelangelo's David and precious stone works

ACCADEMIA GALLERY (P. 32) – MUSEO DELL'OPIFICIO
DELLE PIETRE DURE (P. 62-63)

In via Ricasoli, a long queue of modern-day pilgrims waiting to see *David* usually marks the entrance to the Gallery of the Accademia (no. 58-60). One of the most visited museums in the world, it is housed, together with the Accademia delle Belle Arti, the Cherubini Conservatory and the Opificio delle Pietre Dure, in the former hospital of San Matteo and monastery of San Niccolò di Cafaggio, taking up the entire city block up to via degli Alfani. The Accademia Gallery is often considered 'the Michelangelo Museum' because of the extraordinary sculptures it contains: *David*, the so-called *Prisoners* and *Saint Matthew* (in this regard it seems worthwhile noting that special three-day passes can be purchased for an itinerary devoted to the genus of Michelangelo through the Accademia Gallery, the Bargello National Museum and the Museum of the Medici Chapels). However, the Accademia also houses a unique collection of gold-back paintings from the 15th and 16th centuries, as well as significant collections of plaster casts from the 19th Century, Russian icons, and musical instruments. Although some of these are temporarily on display in the Room of the Colossus, a permanent exhibition will be set up in four rooms of the adjoining Luigi Cherubini Conservatory, where they will go to institute an interesting separate section of the Accademia. Exiting the gallery to the left, just a few yards along via degli Alfani, at no. 78 is the Museum of the Opificio delle Pietre Dure. Here you can retrace the three-hundred-year artistic endeavours of this unique artisan institution, established by will of grand duke Ferdinando I in 1588, whose exquisite precious stone creations have been admired in the royal courts of all Europe.

Faith and charity about the square of Santissima Annunziata

Santissima Annunziata (p. 169) – Pinacoteca dello Spedale degli Innocenti (p. 130) – National Archaeology Museum (p. 44)

The harmonious Piazza della Santissima Annunziata encircled by rhythmic arcades is one of the most beautiful in Florence for its unified, balanced and serene renaissance character, much of which is owed to Brunelleschi. It was in fact he who built the loggia of the Spedale degli Innocenti (on the right facing the church), which was later complemented by the Loggiato dei Serviti (on the left), initiated in 1516 by Antonio da Sangallo il Vecchio and Baccio d'Agnolo, and finally the church portico, which was added in 1600. It is framed by these architectural theatre curtains that, by looking towards via de' Servi (that is, towards the Cathedral dome), one may best appreciate the view of the equestrian monument to grand duke Ferdinando in the centre of the square. Giambologna began this sculpture late in life and left its completion to Pietro Tacca, who also carried out the two flanking fountains with sea monsters. From the religious, cultural, social and economic perspectives, this square has played an important role in the history of the city. After taking in the overview, your visit proper should begin with the church of Santissima Annunziata, a cherished sanctuary for the Florentines and amongst the oldest and most revered in Tuscany. Its history is tied to the miraculous image of the *Annunciation* that is still jealously guarded here, and by virtue of which the church became such a venerated place of worship, earning rich decorations and precious votive offerings. Next on the itinerary is the Spedale degli Innocenti, the charitable institute for foundlings and symbol of Florence's humanist tradition. The first cloister, called Chiostro degli Uomini (Cloister of Men) is well worth the visit, as is the picture gallery situated in the hall overlying Brunelleschi's portico. Exiting into the square, take via della Colonna on the right to arrive at the National Archaeology Museum, a fundamental institution for the study of Etruscan civilisation.

Palace hopping

This itinerary will take you along the streets of the elegant shopping area in the historic centre, through some of the many mansions found here and into the church of Santa Trinita. Looming large in via della Vigna Nuova is the façade of Palazzo Rucellai. The façade was added by Giovanni di Paolo Rucellai to unify the pre-existing family apartments, together with the front loggia, built to glorify joyous family events and make them public, as was the custom in many 15ᵗʰ-century noble Florentine families. Both these structures were designed by Leon Battista Alberti, the same architect commissioned by the Rucellai for the façade of nearby Santa Maria Novella and the shrine of the Holy Sepulchre, which can be reached from here by walking along the left side of Palazzo Rucellai in via de' Palchetti, then turning right into via de' Federighi, thereby arriving in the square where the church of San Pancrazio once stood, today the museum of the sculptor Marino Marini (1901-1980). Just next to this is the Rucellai chapel (entry in via della Spada), the harmonious marble shrine designed by Alberti in the same proportions as the Church of the Holy Sepulchre in Jerusalem. Continuing to the right along via della Spada you will come to via Tornabuoni, where just opposite to the right is Palazzo Strozzi. By walking along this building's side up to the square of the same name (piazza Strozzi), one can better appreciate its imposing, yet elegant architecture, symbol of the power and wealth of Filippo Strozzi, who entrusted its construction to Benedetto da Maiano in 1489. Currently, it is the headquarters of important cultural institutions and although it often hosts temporary exhibitions, it is not generally open to the pub-

lic. In any event, its courtyard can be visited and is well worth a look. Back again in the square, take the first right, via Monalda, to emerge in via Porta Rossa, where at no. 13 you may enter Palazzo Davanzati to view its interior (only the ground floor until ongoing work has been completed), as it currently houses the Museo della Casa Fiorentina antica (Museum of the ancient Florentine Home). After touring the museum, continue left up to piazza Santa Trinita, an irregular crossroad in whose centre you will see the granite column (brought here from the Thermal baths of Caracalla in Rome), atop which Romolo del Tadda placed the porphyry statue of *Justice* in 1581. Here, in a strategic position near the Santa Trinita bridge, stands the late 13th-century Palazzo Spini (later palazzo Feroni), which although remodelled a number of times, still preserves an austere, embattled aspect, especially in its crowning. The church of Santa Trinita with its Vallombrosan convent was founded in the early 11th Century. In the Sassetti chapel within, one of the frescoes done by Domenico Ghirlandaio shows how the square looked in the late 15th Century. In front of the church, a bit to the left, at no. 1 is Palazzo Bartolini Salimbeni, designed in the classical Roman style that Baccio di Agnolo imported from the Italian capital in about 1520. Also after Roman models is the baroque architecture of Palazzo Corsini, the last stop, chronologically as well as physically, in this itinerary. To reach it, continue up to the Arno and then go right along the river up to no. 10. The paintings, part of one of the most important private collections in Florence, are displayed on the first floor, which maintains its original layout.

Oltrarno

Set on the river's left bank, the Oltrarno (literally, 'beyond the Arno') is a popular town quarter whose colourful atmosphere has been immortalised in writing by Vasco Pratolini and in painting by Ottone Rosai. The district's residents are proud to live a near separate existence from the rest of the city. Traditionally an area populated with artisans, numerous age-old, and ever rarer, crafts are still practised here, handed down from generation to generation. The itinerary begins at the church of Santa Maria del Carmine, whose bare façade hides the secret treasure contained along the right aisle within – the Brancacci Chapel. The entrance to this recently restored chapel is to the right of the church façade, then through the silent cloister and Chapter House. The frescoes here were done by Masolino and Masaccio, while the chapel was completed by Filippino Lippi over half century later. The decorations represent the point of departure for modern painting, and therefore a cardinal reference in the history of art. Returning to the square, go right into via Santa Monaca and once again in via Sant'Agostino to arrive in piazza Santo Spirito, nowadays a lively centre of local activities. The church of Santo Spirito is the very symbol of the Oltrarno quarter. Its stately architecture, designed by Brunelleschi, was once admired by Michelangelo and held by Bernini to be the most beautiful in the world. There are many splendid masterpieces to be viewed here, and many of the chapels off the left aisle preserve their original fifteenth-century arrangements, made up of an altarpiece with its *predella* and *palio*. Once you have exited, turn right to find the refectory of Santo Spirito (no. 29), one of the less frequently visited sites in the city, but all the more suggestive for this very reason, and in any event, well worth the stop to admire the frescoes by Andrea di Cione (known as Orcagna) and the many works of art donated to the city by the antiquarian Salvatore Romano.

Then, taking the short via de' Michelozzi, you will come out into via Maggio, the main road that the grand dukes once traversed in their carriages on the way out of Pitti Palace and where today antiquarians in the historic buildings lining the street display the tokens of glorious times past. Walking along in the direction of the Arno, then turning right into Borgo San Jacopo, where several tower houses saved from the devastation of the second world war line the way, you will arrive at the left side of Ponte Vecchio. Originally, this was the point at which the two shores of the Arno were closest, and therefore the earliest, wooden bridge was erected here in the First Century BC. This was followed by a masonry structure, destroyed in the great flood of 1333, when the current bridge was built. Until the late 16th Century the shops on the bridge were occupied by butchers', fishmongers', cobblers' and blacksmiths'. However, after Vasari constructed the corridor for the grand duke to cross from Palazzo Vecchio to Pitti Palace in 1565, the din and smell emanating from the shops prompted Ferdinando I to replace such activities with goldsmiths' in 1593. The goldsmiths were forced by decree to move into the picturesque shops along the bridge, which has since been all the more silent and all the more cherished. By following precisely Varsari's corridor as it circumvents the tower of the Mannelli family (which refused to be humbled by having their tower traversed), then passes over via de' Bardi and enters amongst the buildings to finally flank the façade of Santa Felicita, you will come to this jewel of a church containing Pontormo's masterpiece. The last stop in this walk can be reached by taking via de' Bardi, once known as Borgo Pitiglioso (i.e., the lousy quarter). Here, the Bardini Museum at piazza de' Mozzi no. 1 houses the collection donated by the antiquarian Stefano Bardini to the Township of Florence in 1922.

The royal palace

PITTI PALACE (P. 100-101)

Dominating the underlying square is the façade of Pitti Palace, Florence's most imposing and monumental building, behind which extend Boboli Gardens. Visiting this regal palace and the prestigious collections contained therein is to retrace the history of the three dynasties (the Medici, Lorraine and Savoys) that it has housed. It is in fact the seat of important museums of the fine and applied arts. We may start out with the Palatine Gallery on the first floor of the left wing, whose entrance is through the courtyard staircase to the right. Its rooms maintain all the appeal of the original ducal collection, whose paintings are arranged according to aesthetic criteria in richly sculpted and gilded frames under opulently frescoed vaults. Paintings from the 15th to 17th centuries, including the work of Raphael and Andrea del Sarto, make up the greatest part of the core collection. The Venetian school, especially Titian, is also well represented. After the Gallery, our path continues on the first floor of the right wing, in the Royal Apartments, the entrance fee to which is included in the Gallery ticket. The rooms of the so-called Tapestries Apartments then follow, where the ceilings bear the building's oldest decorations (early17th Century). Then on the second floor are the thirty rooms given over to the Modern Art Gallery whose holdings covers a broad time span from the years of Pietro Leopoldo up to the first world war. The ground floor 'summer apartments' hold the Silverworks Museum, which can be visited, together with the Porcelain Museum in the Knight's Lodge on the hilltop in Boboli Gardens, by purchasing a single ticket for both. Within Boboli Gardens you will see the main façade of the Meridian Building, a neo-classic construction from the late 18th Century, now given over to the Costume Museum, that documents the evolution of fashion from the 18th Century up to the first decades of the 20th Century. Lastly, the Carriage Museum on the right-side of the ground floor facing the façade should be noted (although it is generally closed). It is devoted for the most part to exhibition of the carriages belonging to the Lorraine and Savoy houses. And to conclude the visit, enter Boboli Gardens, a true open-air museum (including therefore an entrance fee). The setting is an exceptional example of the Italian-style garden, with fountains, grottoes and sculptures immersed in lush greenery. At any time of the year, the visitor will be rewarded with moments of quiet introspection stirred by the gardens' unique vistas.

The best view in town

SAN MINIATO AL MONTE (P. 151) — FORTE BELVEDERE (P. 189)

This itinerary is a salute to Florence as seen from atop the tall hills surrounding it on the Arno's left bank. Because of the distances (and gradients) involved, it is best completed with some means of transportation. Our route unwinds along viale dei Colli, planned by the architect Giuseppe Poggi, who also engineered the city's ring road on commission to the Township during the urban renewal project begun when Florence became capital of the Kingdom of Italy (1865-1871). From the square of piazza Francesco Ferrucci, we follow viale Michelangelo, actually the first segment of viale dei Colli, up to piazzale Michelangelo, which offers a splendid view overlooking the city. The monument to Michelangelo, also by Poggi (1871), is made up of a bronze copy of *David* surrounded by copies of the statues adorning the Medici tombs in the New Sacristy of San Lorenzo. The loggia behind (today a café) had also been planned as a homage to Michelangelo: according to Poggi's original design, it was supposed to have housed sculptures by the great artist. The itinerary continues with a visit to the Romanesque church of San Miniato al Monte, a masterpiece of Florentine architecture. It is located just up the road; in fact, on the left its façade is visible on top of the monumental staircase, also designed by Poggi. Then continuing along viale Galileo Galilei and turning right into via San Leonardo, we reach Fort Belvedere. A walk along via San Leonardo is well worth the effort, as it is bordered by plastered and graffito decorated walls, villas, olive groves and cypresses. Just before Porta San Giorgio on the left is the main entrance to Fort Belvedere, a fortress wedged into the city fabric, which offers a breath-taking view of Florence's monuments, so near that you will feel almost able to touch them, one by one.

An eclectic collector

STIBBERT MUSEUM (P. 98-99)

The Stibbert Museum is one of the 'added attractions' proposed here, together with the Cenacolo di San Salvi, for those who wish to go beyond the usual tourist-beaten path. Some means of transportation is advisable for this itinerary as well. We begin in piazza della Libertà, where the San Gallo city gate bears testimony to the medieval city walls just opposite the triumphal arch erected on the occasion of the solemn entry of Francesco Stefano of Lorraine in 1739. From here, cross the Mugnone stream, then take via Vittorio Emanuele II, and after the second railway crossing turn right into via Stibbert, which skirts the first section of the garden park of the nineteenth-century villa Fabbricotti. We thus come to no. 26, the entrance to the Stibbert Museum, housed in the villa constituted by the union of a number of buildings erected between 1879 and 1891. It was here that the Englishman, Frederick Stibbert, amassed his private collection, mostly of ancient weapons and uniforms, and remodelled the villa's interior as a museum for its exhibition. It is therefore a museum to be seen, not only for the size and uniqueness of its collection, but also for the suggestiveness of the settings in which the works are exhibited. The large park surrounding the villa also underscores the eclecticism of Stibbert's tastes: it combines the tradition English garden with an Egyptian style shrine, a Greek temple and a ceramic-faced loggia.

A monastery without the walls

CENACOLO DI SAN SALVI (P. 178)

This itinerary (once again it is best to have some means of transportation), takes us into the north-eastern area of the city, well beyond the city walls of the "di qua d'Arno", that is, "this side of the Arno". In order to fulfil the needs of a 'modern' city when Florence was designated capital of the Kingdom of Italy (1865-1871), this part of the city walls was demolished on a project by the architect Giuseppe Poggi and replaced by wide boulevards on the Parisian model, interspersed with squares around the city gates, which were fortunately spared from the devastation. We begin at one of these, Porta la Croce (Gate of the Cross) in piazza Beccaria, whence we start up viale Edmondo De Amicis, and passing the railway, take the third right, via Tito Speri, which leads to the ancient church of San Michele a San Salvi. In 1048, this church and convent were donated to Giovanni Gualberto, founder of the Vallombrosan order. On the right, in via di San Salvi no. 16, is the entrance to the refectory of Andrea del Sarto, since 1981 a museum housed within the ex-convent's quarters. Here, as its name implies, you will be able to view, not only sculptures and paintings by the 16th-century Florentine artist, but above all his fresco of the *Last Supper* on the rear wall of the refectory. It is a work of such extraordinary quality that it was spared by Charles V during the siege of Florence in 1530.

USEFUL INFORMATION

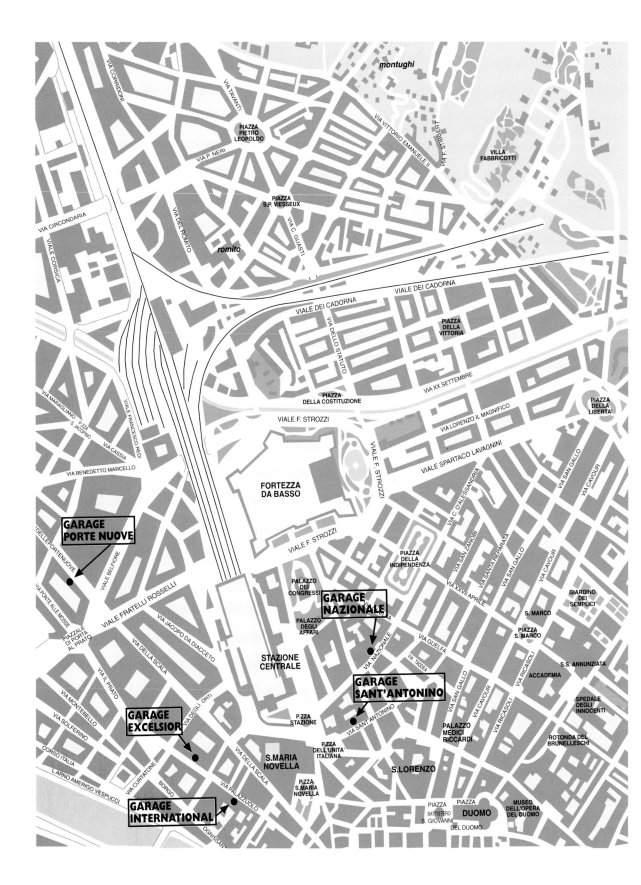

CAR PARKS

Car parks for convenient access to the historic centre:

Garage Excelsior
via Palazzuolo, 94 - Tel. 055.215100 Fax 055.215140
Open 06.00-02.00 including holidays
Cas washed by hand
Pickup service available at major hotels: Hotel Excelsior, Grand Hotel, Villa Medici

Garage International
via Palazzuolo 29 - Tel. 055.282386 Fax 055.2381583
Open 07.00-24.00
Car wash
Bicycles at customer's disposal
Hotel pickup service

Garage Nazionale
via Nazionale 21 - Tel. e Fax 055.284041
Open 06.00-24.00 Mon.-Fri.
07.00-12.00/18.00-22.00 Sundays
Hotel pickup service

Garage Porte Nuove
via Porte Nuove 21 - Tel. 055.333355 Fax 055.332876
Open 07.00-02.00 including holidays
Car wash
Road assistence

Garage Sant'Antonino
via S. Antonino 13r - Tel. e Fax 055.210490
Open 07.00-23.00 including holidays

TIMETABLE

Cappella Brancacci, Church of Santa Maria del Carmine, piazza del Carmine 14, tel. 055-2382195. Closed: Tuesdays, January 1 & 7, Easter Sunday, May 1, July 16, August 15, December 25.

Cappella dei Magi, Palazzo Medici-Riccardi, via Cavour 1. Information and bookings: tel. 055-2760340. Closed: Wednesdays, January 1, December 25. Groups of 15 are admitted every quarter hour.

Cenacolo "di Fuligno", via Faenza 40-42. Tel. 055-286982. Closed: January 1, May 1, December 25.

Cenacolo di Ognissanti, Borgo Ognissanti 42. Tel. 055-2396802. Open: Mondays, Tuesdays and Saturdays 9-12.

Cenacolo di San Salvi, via di San Salvi 16. Tel. 055-2388603. Accessible to the handicapped. Closed: Mondays, January 1, May 1, December 25.

Cenacolo di Sant'Apollonia, via XXVII Aprile 1. Tel. 055-2388607. Accessible to the handicapped. Closed: 2nd and 4th Monday of each month; 1st, 3rd and 5th Sunday of each month; January 1, May 1, December 25.

Cenacolo di Santo Spirito, piazza Santo Spirito 29. Tel. 055-287043. Accessible to the handicapped. Closed: Mondays, January 1, Easter Sunday, May 1, August 15, December 25.

Chiostro dello Scalzo, via Cavour 69. Tel. 055-2388604. Open: Mondays and Thursdays 9-13. For information contact Firenze Musei, tel. 055-294883, fax 055-264406, Monday to Friday 8.30-18.30, Saturday 8.30-12.30 (answer phone operative at other times).

Galleria d'arte moderna (Modern Art Gallery), Pitti Palace, piazza Pitti. Tel. 055-2388616-2388601, fax 055-2654520. Accessible to the handicapped. Closed: 1st, 3rd and 5th Monday and 2nd and 4th Sunday of each month; January 1, May 1, December 25. For information and bookings contact Firenze Musei, tel. 055-294883, fax 055-264406, Monday to Friday 8.30-18.30, Saturday 8.30-12.30 (answer phone operative at other times).

Galleria degli Uffizi, piazzale degli Uffizi, tel. 055-2388651-2388652; fax 055-2388699. Web site: http://musa.uffizi.firenze.it. Accessible to the handicapped. For information and bookings contact Firenze Musei, tel. 055-294883, fax 055-264406, Monday to Friday 8.30-18.30, Saturday 8.30-12.30 (answer phone operative at other times).

Galleria del Costume, Pitti Palace, piazza Pitti. Tel. 055-2388713. Closed: 1st, 3rd and 5th Monday and 2nd and 4th Sunday of each month; January 1, May 1, December 25. For information and bookings contact Firenze Musei, tel. 055-294883, fax 055-264406, Monday to Friday 8.30-18.30, Saturday 8.30-12.30 (answer phone operative at other times).

Galleria dell'Accademia (Accademia Gallery), via Ricasoli 58-60. Administrative offices: tel. 055-2388609. Information: tel. 055-2388612. Accessible to the handicapped. Closed: Mondays, January 1, May 1, December 25. For information and bookings contact Firenze Musei, tel. 055-294883, fax 055-264406, Monday to Friday 8.30-18.30, Saturday 8.30-12.30 (answer phone operative at other times).

Galleria di Palazzo Corsini, via del Parione 11. Tel. 055-218994. Visits by booking only.

Galleria Palatina and Appartamenti Reali (Palatine Gallery and Royal Apartments), Palazzo Pitti, piazza Pitti. Tel.055-2388611-2388614, fax 055-2388613. Accessible to the handicapped. Closed: Mondays, January 1, May 1, December 25. From January 7 to March 31 the Royal Apartments are open only for group and school visits booked in advance. For information and bookings contact Firenze Musei, tel. 055-294883, fax 055-264406, Monday to Friday 8.30-18.30, Saturday 8.30-12.30 (answer phone operative at other times).

Giardino di Boboli (Boboli Gardens) Pitti Palace, piazza Pitti. Closed: Mondays, January 1, May 1, December 25. For information and bookings contact Firenze Musei, tel. 055-294883, fax 055-264406, Monday to Friday 8.30-18.30, Saturday 8.30-12.30 (answer phone operative at other times).

Museo Archeologico Nazionale (National Archaeology Museum), via della Colonna 38. Administrative offices: tel. 055-23575, fax 055-242213. Accessible to the handicapped. Closed: Mondays, January 1, May 1, December 25. For information and bookings contact Firenze Musei, tel. 055-294883, fax 055-264406, Monday to Friday 8.30-18.30, Saturday 8.30-12.30 (answer phone operative at other times).

Museo Bardini (Bardini Museum), piazza de'Mozzi 1. Tel. 055-2342427. Partially accessible to the handicapped. Closed: Wednesdays, January 1, Easter Sunday, May 1, August 15, December 25.

Museo degli Argenti (Silverworks Museum) Palazzo Pitti, piazza Pitti. Accessible to the handicapped. Tel. 055-2388709, fax 055-2388710. Closed: Mondays, January 1, May 1, December 25.

Museo dell'Opera del Duomo, piazza Duomo 9. Tel. 055-2302885, fax 055-2302898. Accessible to the handicapped. Closed: January 1, Easter Sunday, December 25.

Museo dell'Opera di Santa Croce, piazza Santa Croce 16. Tel. 055-244619, fax 055-2342289. Accessible to the handicapped. Closed: Wednesdays.

Museo dell'Opificio delle Pietre Dure, via degli Alfani 78. Information: tel. 055-218709. Closed: Sundays, January 1, May 1, December 25.

Museo delle Cappelle Medicee (Medici Chapels), piazza Madonna degli Aldobrandini 6, tel. 055-2388602. Closed: 1st, 3rd and 5th Monday and 2nd and 4th Sunday of each month; January 1, May 1, December 25. For information and bookings contact Firenze Musei, tel. 055-294883, fax 055-264406, Monday to Friday 8.30-18.30, Saturday 8.30-12.30 (answer phone operative at other times).

Museo di Casa Buonarroti, via Ghibellina 70. Tel. 055-241752, fax 055-241698. Closed: Tuesdays, January 1, Easter Sunday, April 25, May 1, August 15, December 25.

Museo di San Marco, piazza San Marco 3. Administrative offices: tel. 055-2388608-2388704, fax 055-2388699, Web site: http://www.sbas.firenze.it. Accessible to the handicapped. Closed: 2nd and 4th Monday and 1st, 3rd and 5th Sunday of each month; January 1, May 1, December 25. For information and bookings contact Firenze Musei, tel. 055-294883, fax 055-264406, Monday to Friday 8.30-18.30, Saturday 8.30-12.30 (answer phone operative at other times).

Museo di Santa Maria Novella, piazza Santa Maria Novella 18. Tel. 055-282187. Accessible to the handicapped. Closed: Fridays, January 1, Easter Sunday, May 1, August 15, December 25.

Museo Diocesano di Santo Stefano al Ponte, piazza Santo Stefano al Ponte 5, tel. 055-2710732, fax 055-2710741. Visits by booking only.

Museo Horne (Horne Museum), via de' Benci 6. Tel. 055-244661. Closed: Sunday, January 1, January 6, Easter Sunday, Mondays of the Angelus, May 1, June 24, August 15, November 1, December 8, 25 & 26.

Museo Nazionale del Bargello (Bargello National Museum), via del Proconsolo 4. Administrative offices: tel. 055-2388606, fax 055-2388699, Web site: http://www.sbas.firenze.it. Accessible to the handicapped. Closed: 2nd and 4th Monday and 1st, 3rd and 5th Sunday of each month; January 1, May 1, December 25. For information and bookings contact Firenze Musei, tel. 055-294883, fax 055-264406, Monday to Friday 8.30-18.30, Saturday 8.30-12.30 (answer phone operative at other times).

Museo Stibbert (Stibbert Museum), via Stibbert 26. Tel. 055-475520, fax 055-486049. Accessible to the handicapped. Closed: Thursdays.

Palazzo Davanzati or Museo della Casa Fiorentina Antica (Museum of the Ancient Florentine Home), via Porta 13. Tel. 055-2388610. Partially accessible to the handicapped. Closed: 1st, 3rd and 5th Monday and 2nd and 4th Sunday of each month; January 1, May 1, December 25.

Palazzo Vecchio Quartieri Monumentali (Monumental quarters), piazza della Signoria, tel. 055-2768325. Partially accessible to the handicapped. Closed: Thursdays, January 1, Easter Sunday, May 1, August 15, December 25.

Pinacoteca dello Spedale degli Innocenti, piazza della Santissima Annunziata 12. Tel. 055-2491723. Closed: Wednesdays, January 1, Easter Sunday, May 1, August 15, December 25.

INDICES

INDEX OF ARTISTS

INDEX OF SIGHTS

printed
in april 2000
at Genesi - Città di Castello
for
s i l l a b e